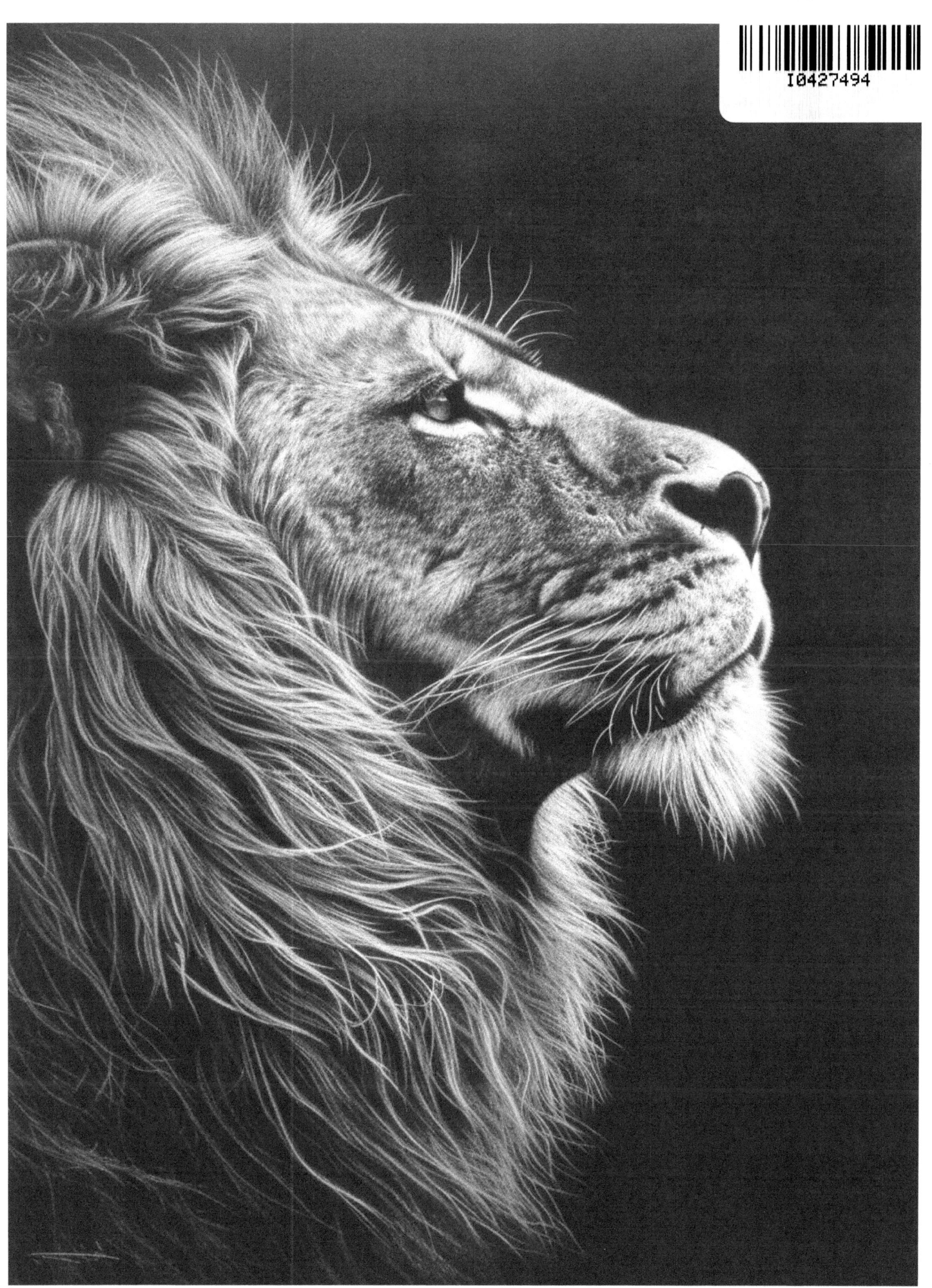

INTRODUCTION

Title: "Royal LIONS: Lionhearted: Capturing Noble Power in Charcoal"
Welcome to "Royal Lions," where the noble essence of these magnificent creatures is brought to life in stunning detail across two volumes.

In this volume, dive into a world of artistic mastery as we present over 100 original designs meticulously crafted in charcoal and graphite pencil media.
This a budget friendly version in comparing to the Vol. 1 which has 225 Lion designs and is intended for anyone that would like to enrich his arsenal of lion designs in a lower budget frame. All the designs are equally carefully selected to be the best they can be for tattoo artists as they are in Vol.1

In this series, lions are more than mere subjects; they are embodiments of regal power and timeless elegance.

Each design is carefully adorned with ornate filigree and baroque ornamentation, symbolizing the royal heritage and indomitable spirit of these majestic animals.

As you explore the pages of "Royal Lions," you'll discover a myriad of poses and expressions, from tranquil repose to fierce determination.

Explore the Lion as a symbol of regal pride and majestic grace.
It reigns as the eternal ruler in the material realm, teaching that true authority transcends the tangible.

Yet, deeper still, the Lion becomes a reflection of the Higher Self, conveying wisdom and nobility beyond words.

Its essence mirrors our potential for greatness, inviting us to embody grace, strength, and wisdom on our journey of self-discovery and mastery

Value beyond Compare: "Royal LIONS" stands as a testament to artistic innovation, delivering a one-of-a-kind resource that saves time, sparks inspiration, and offers unmatched value for money.

With an added 70+ page PDF with the designs of this book, this is more than a book, this is an investment that can return its value 10ths of times only from making 1 tattoo form the content, although there are hundreds of unique and original designs to choose from and do.

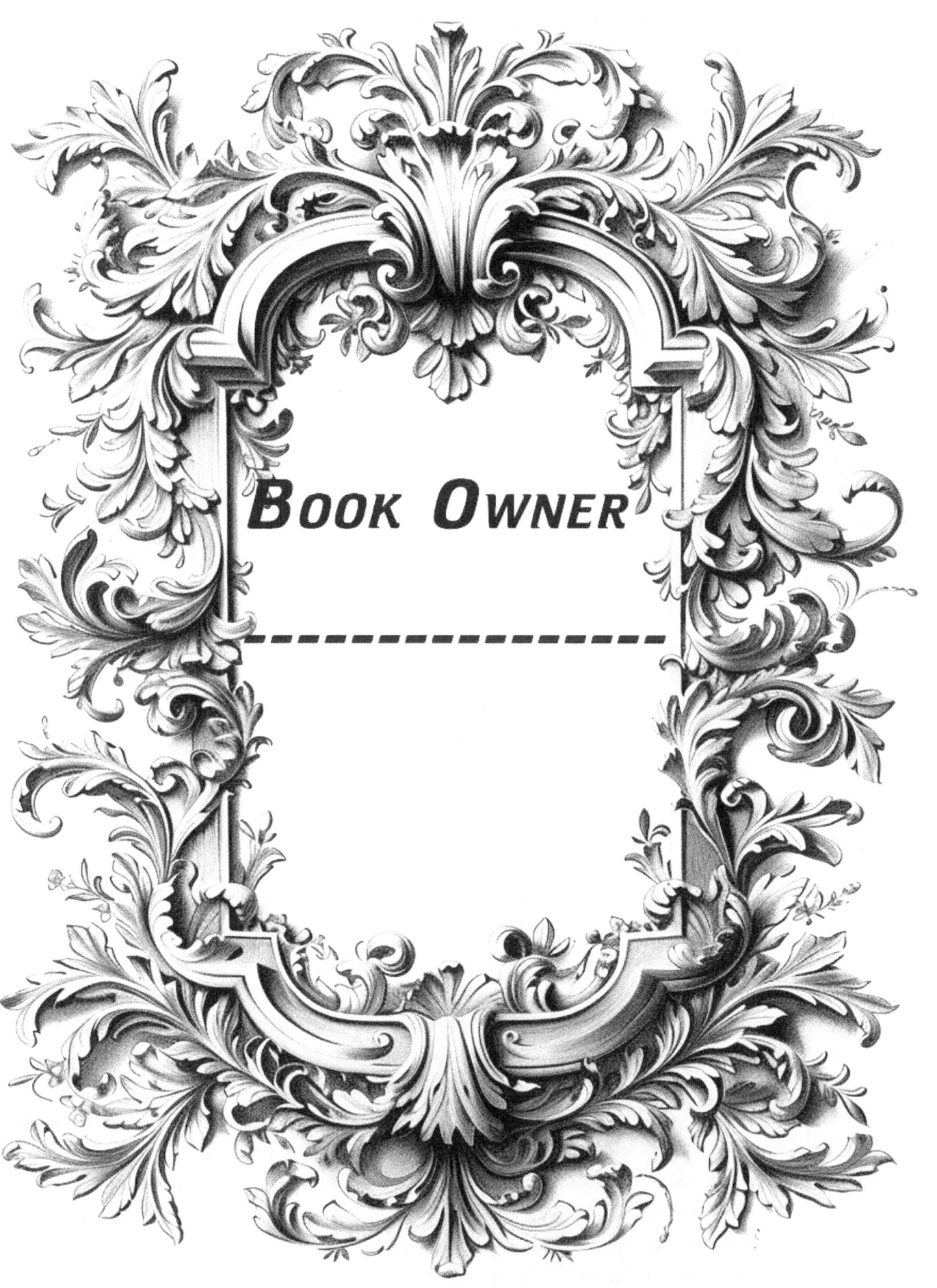

BOOK OWNER

COPYRIGHT

See more of my books here :

amazon.com/author/alexartbooks

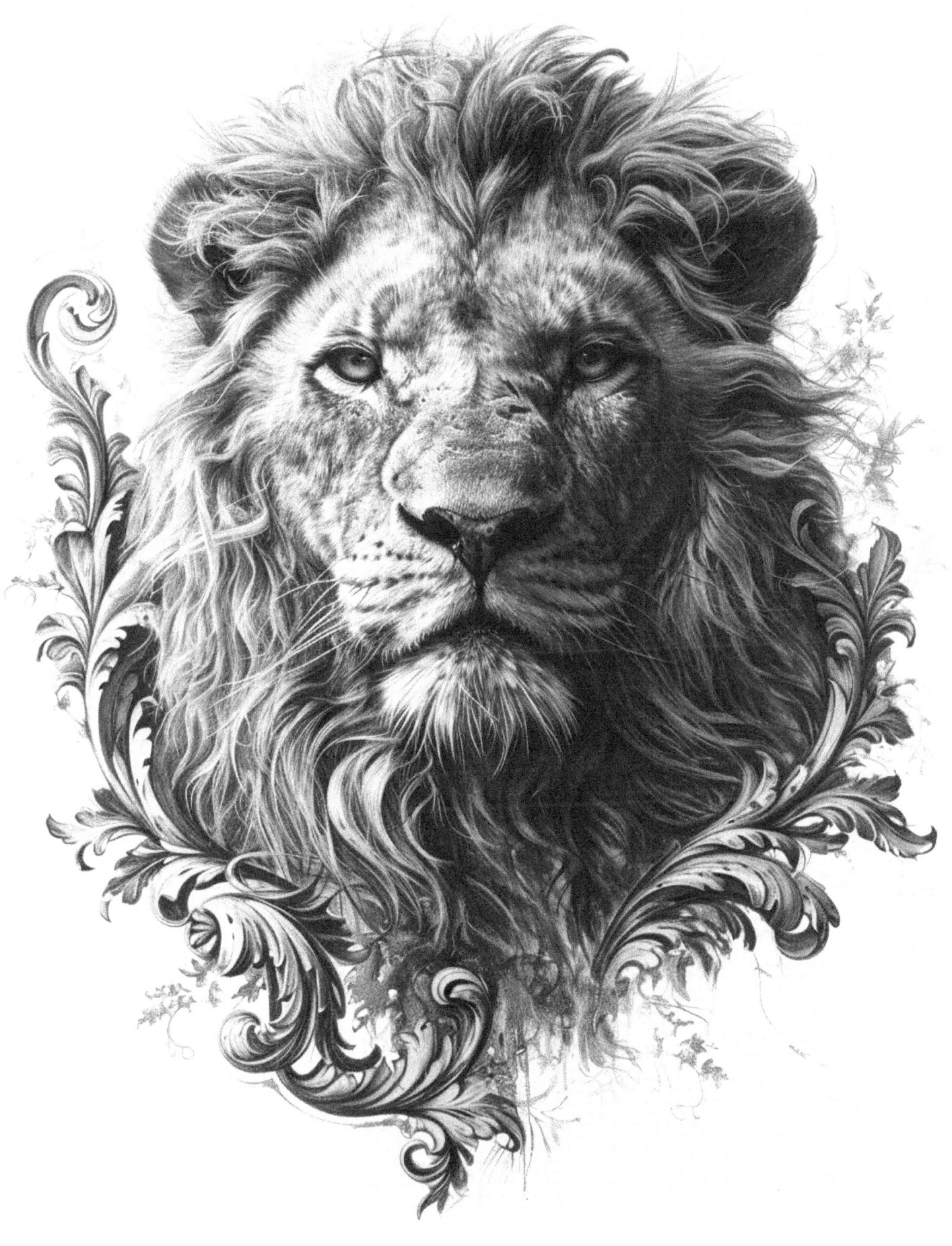

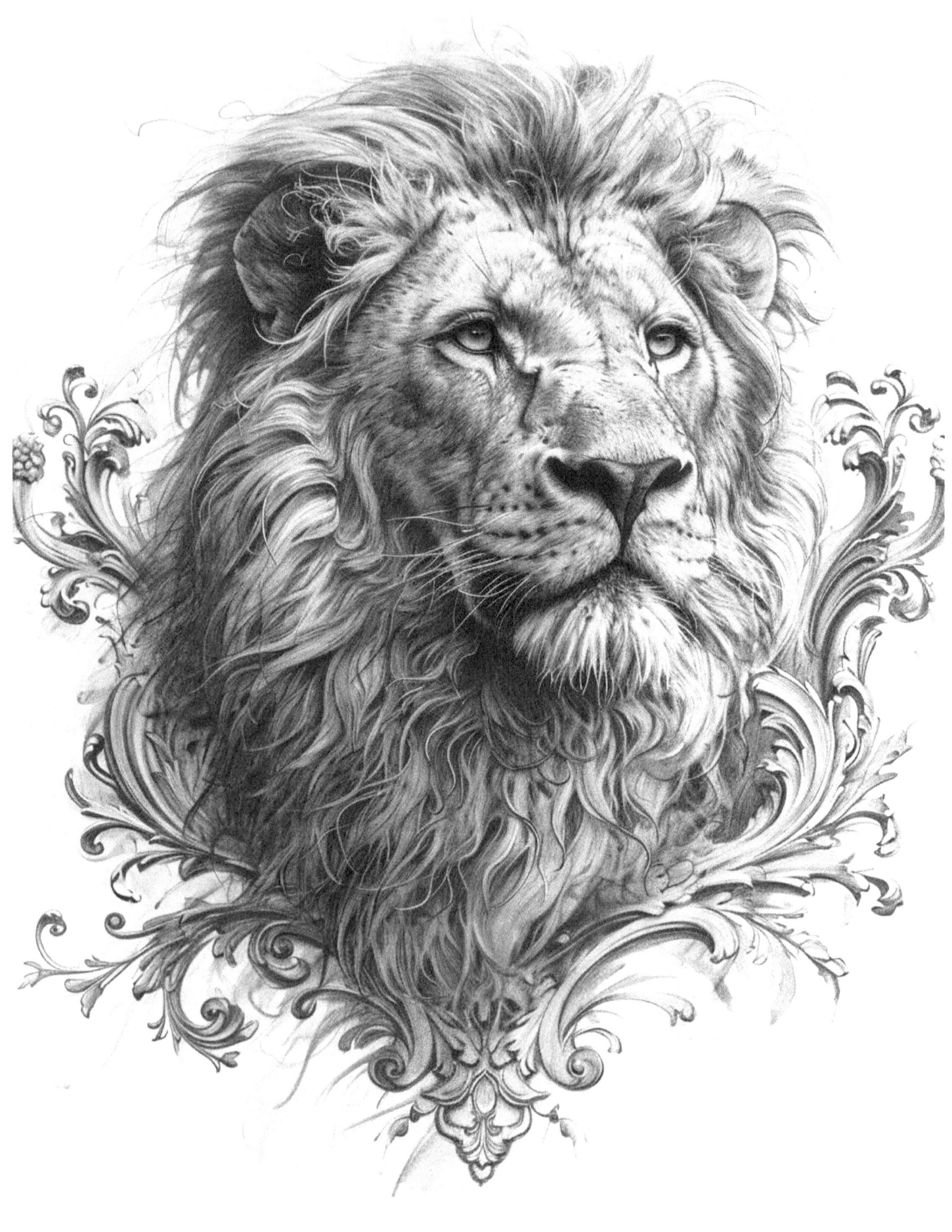

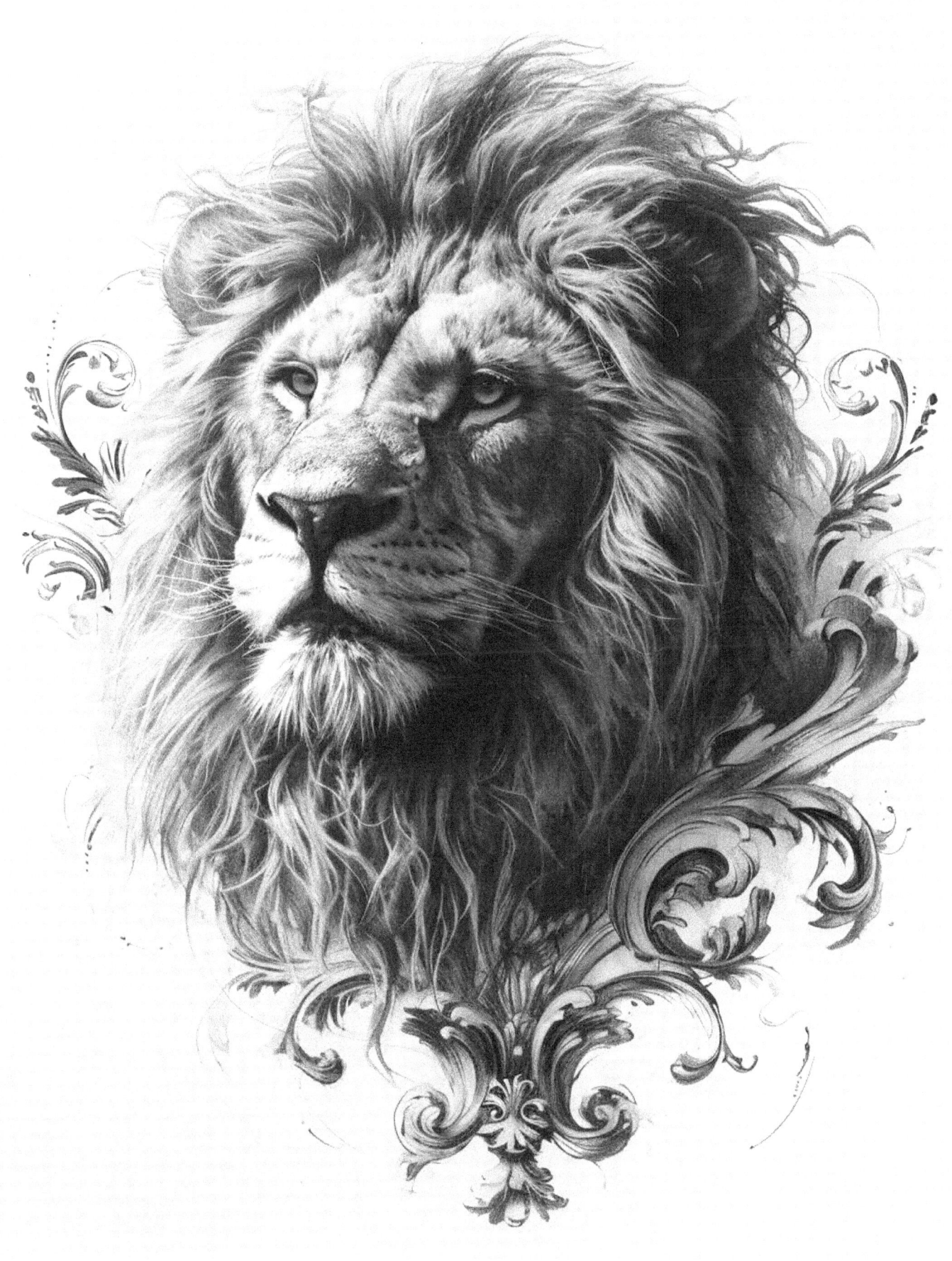

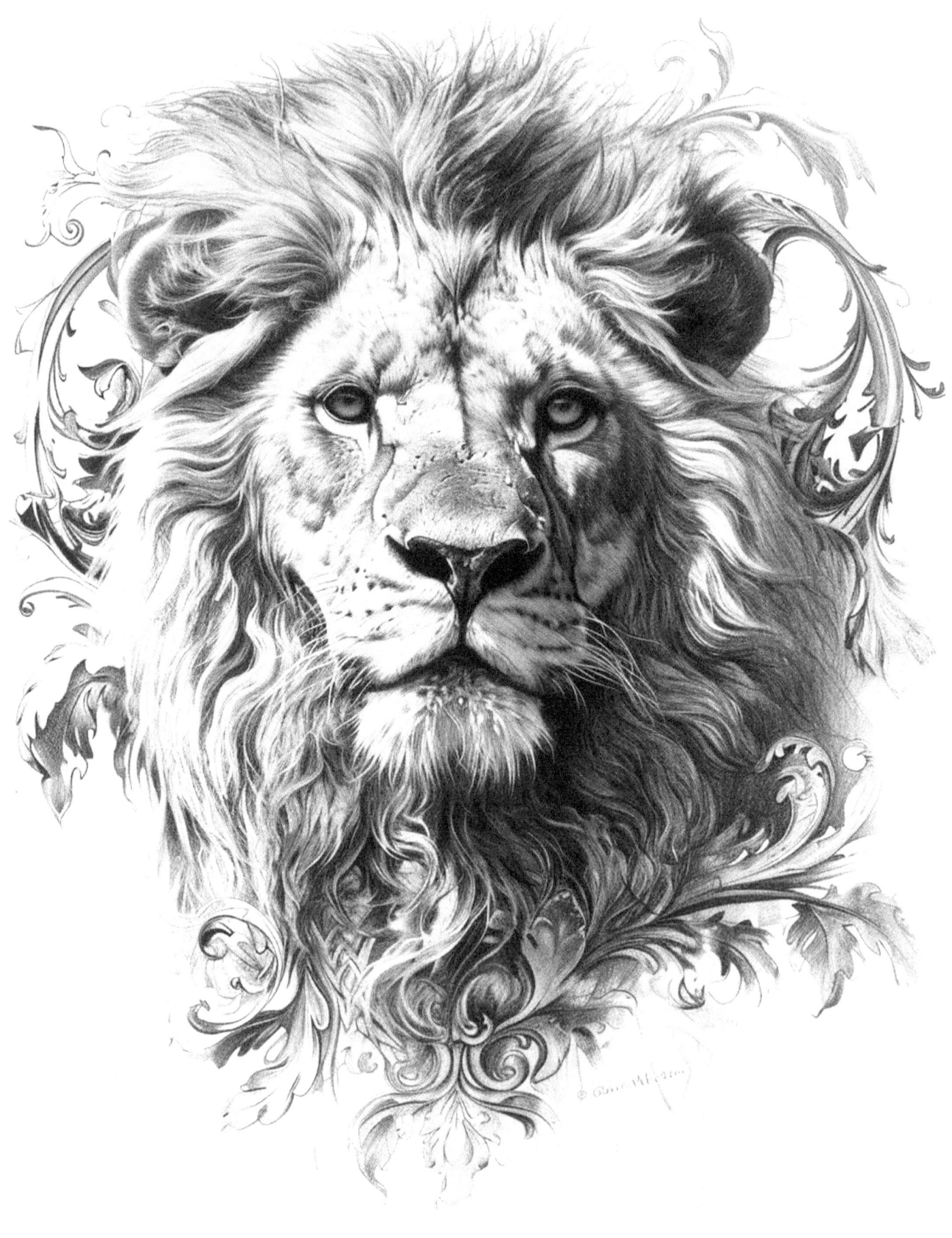

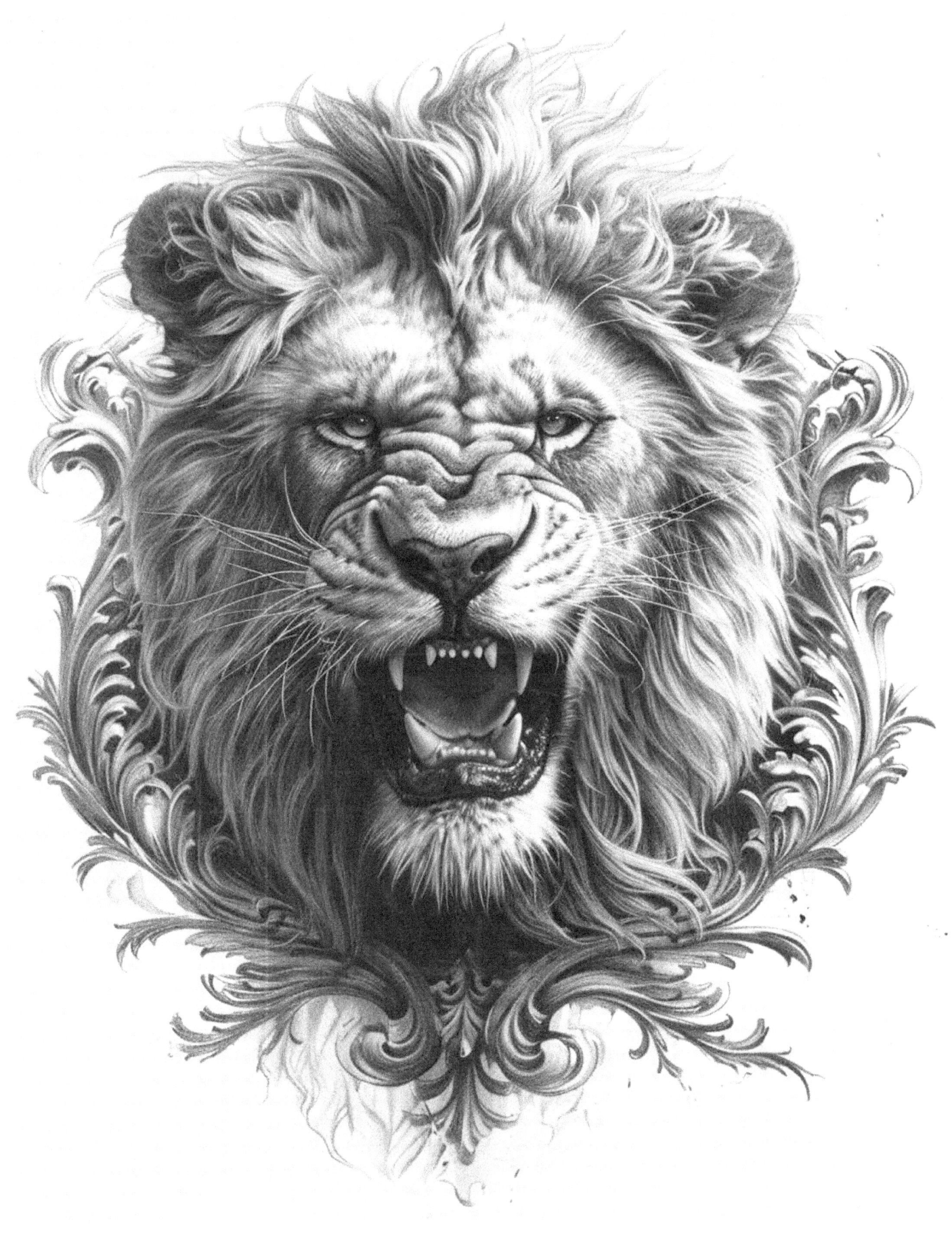

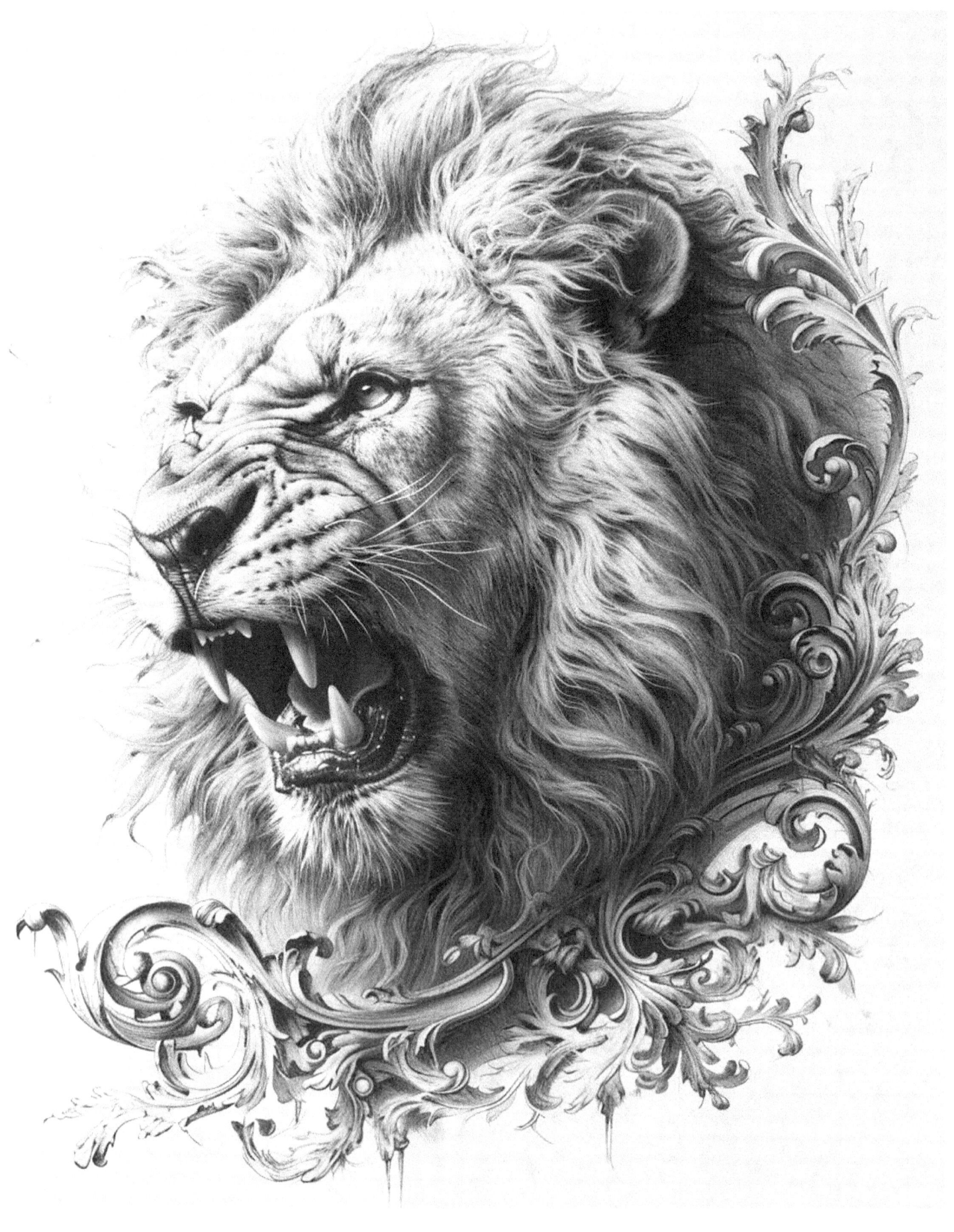

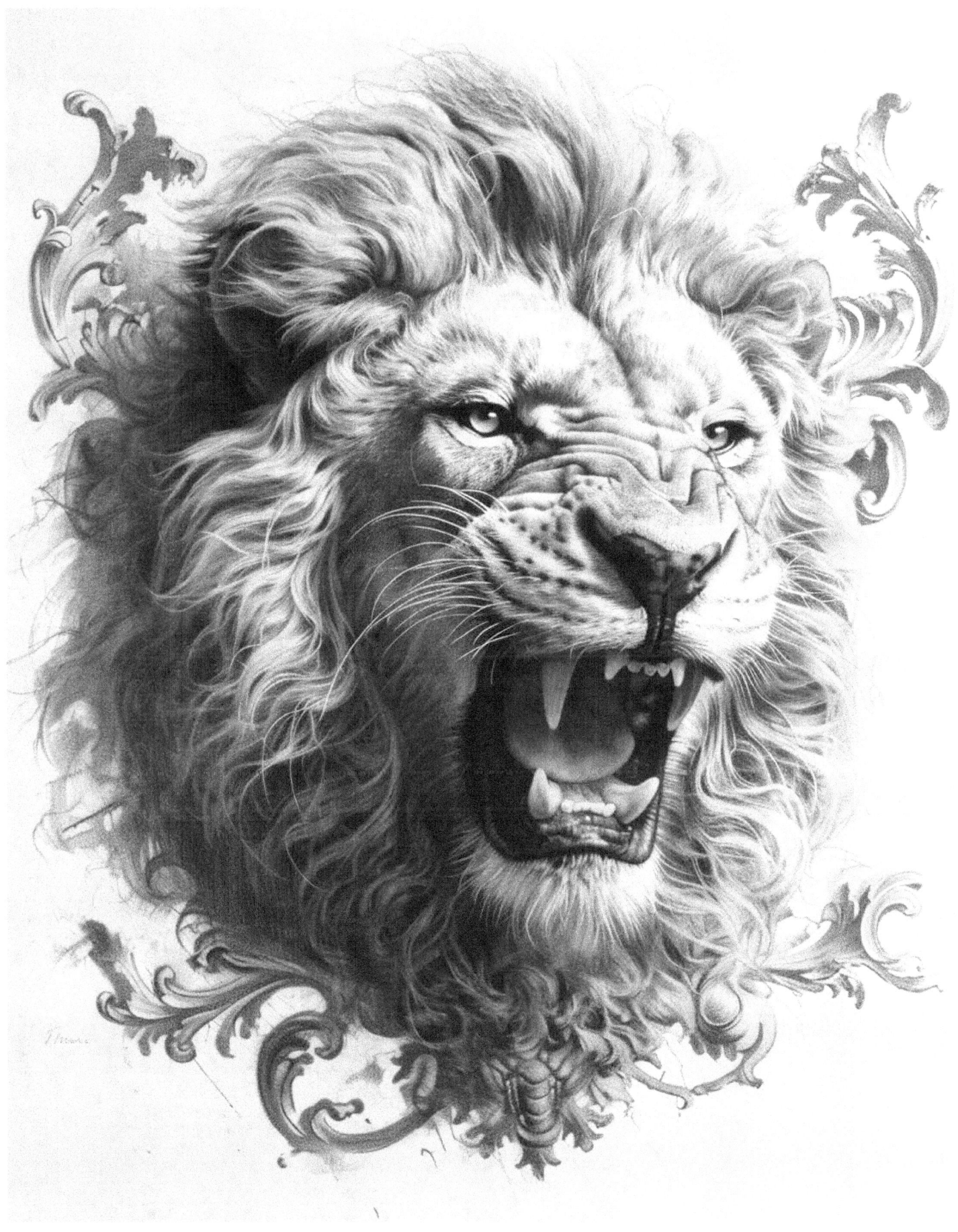

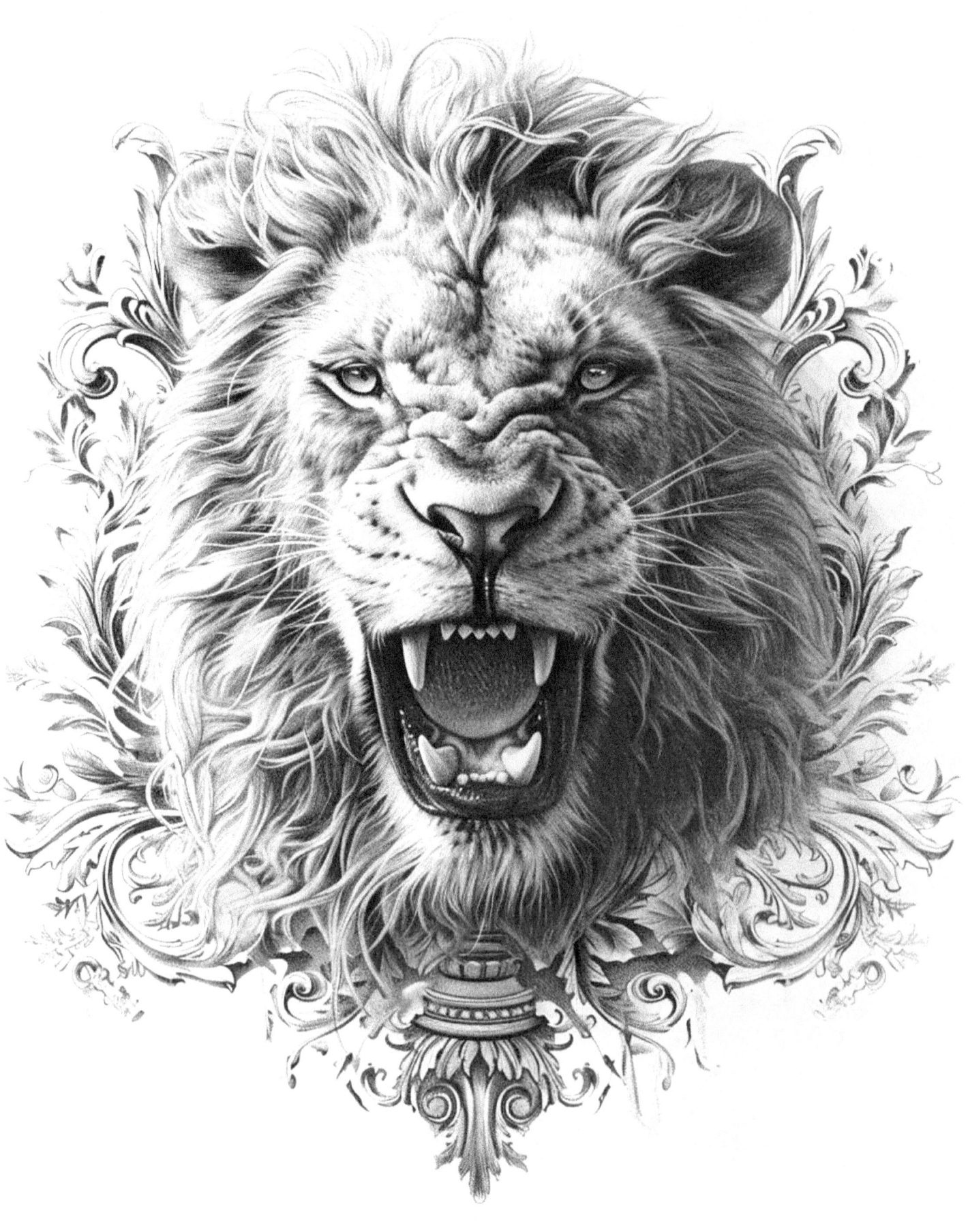

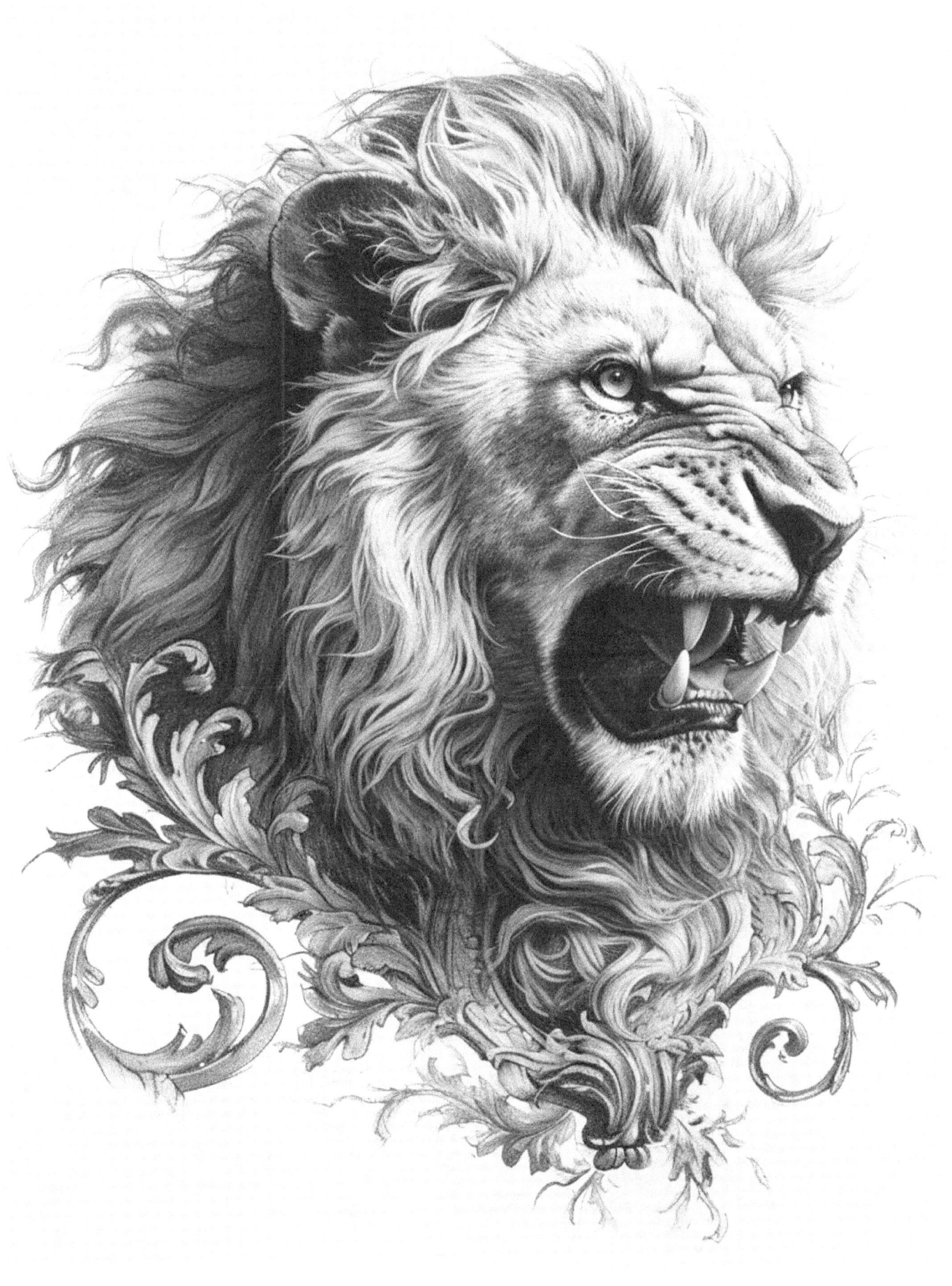

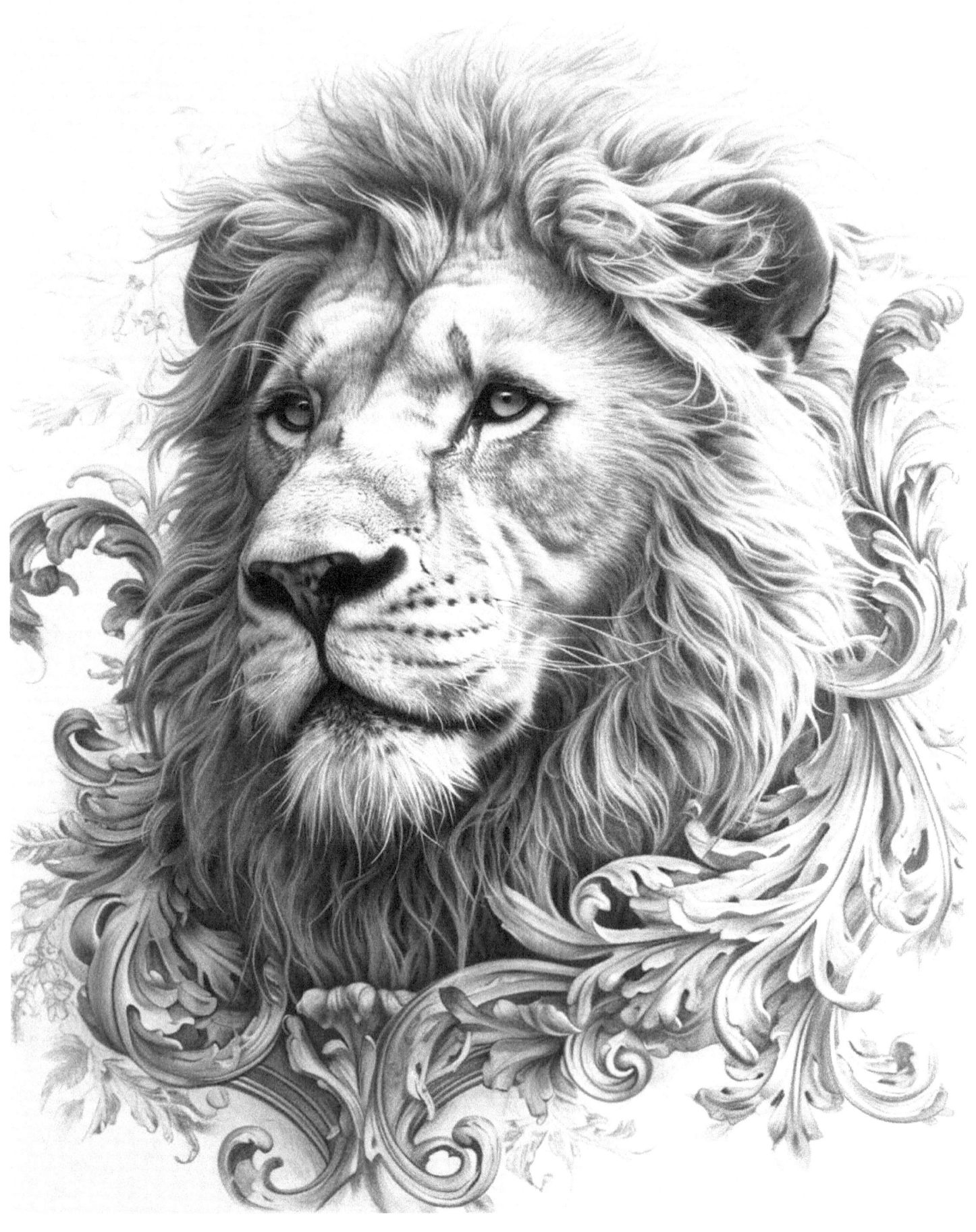

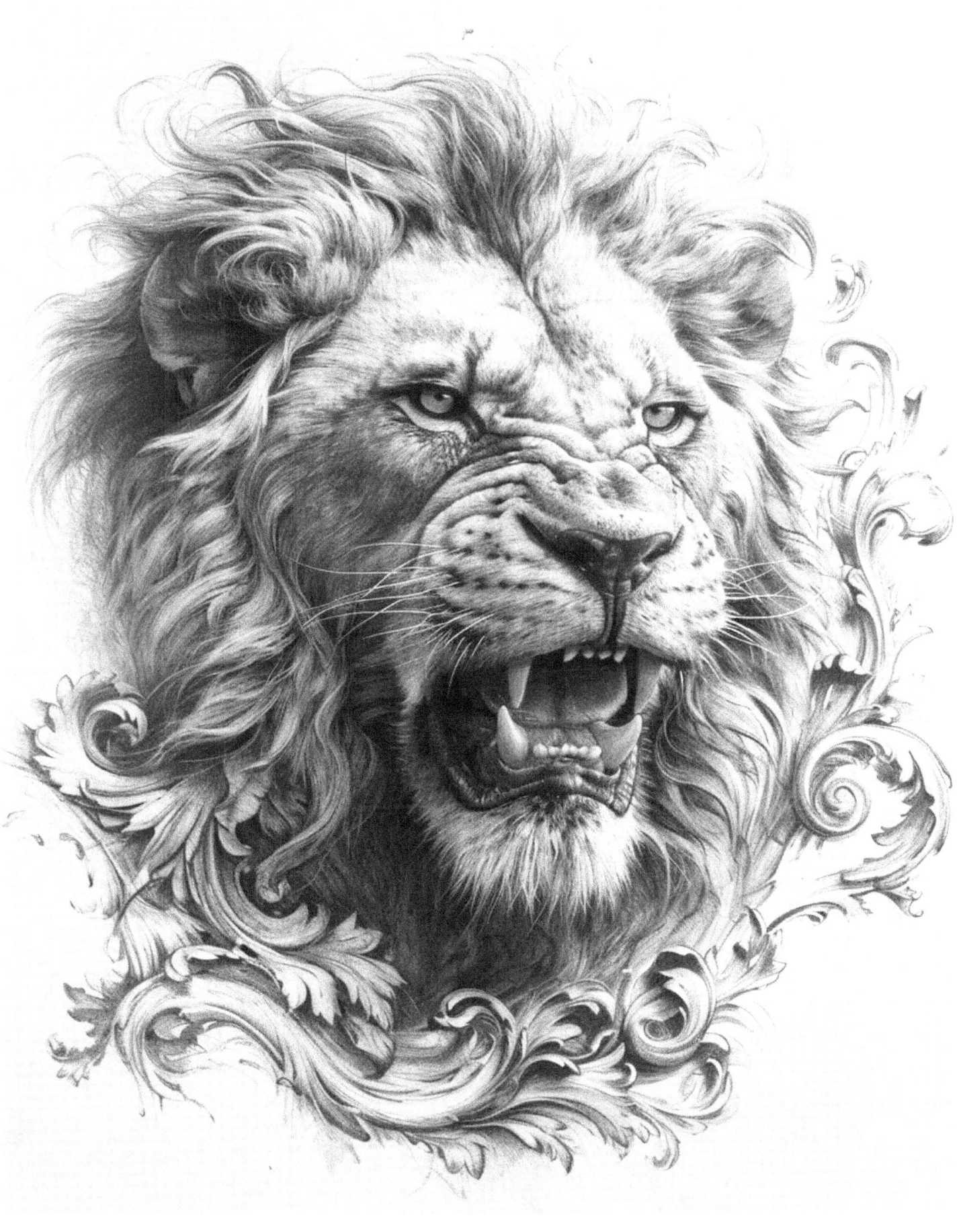

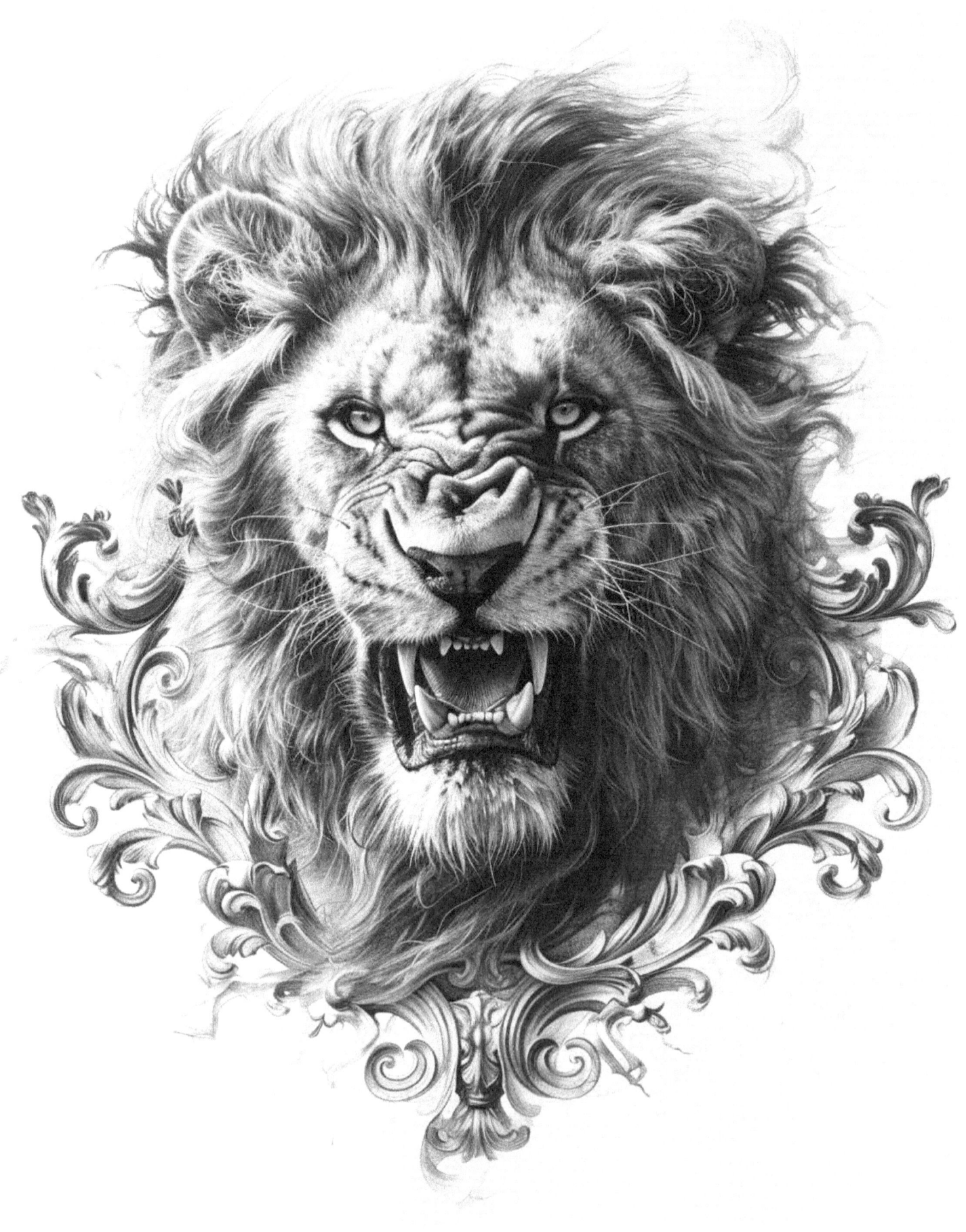

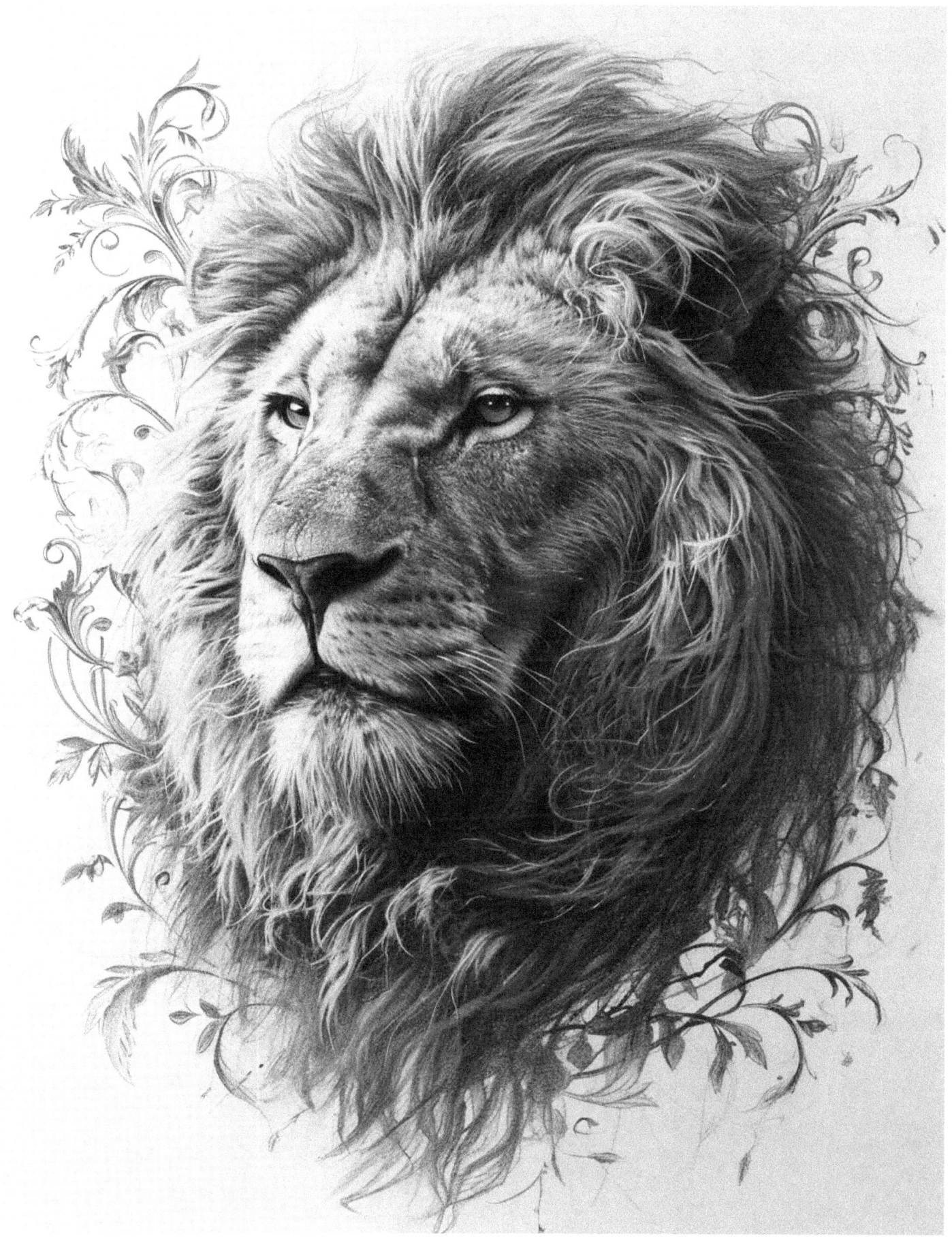

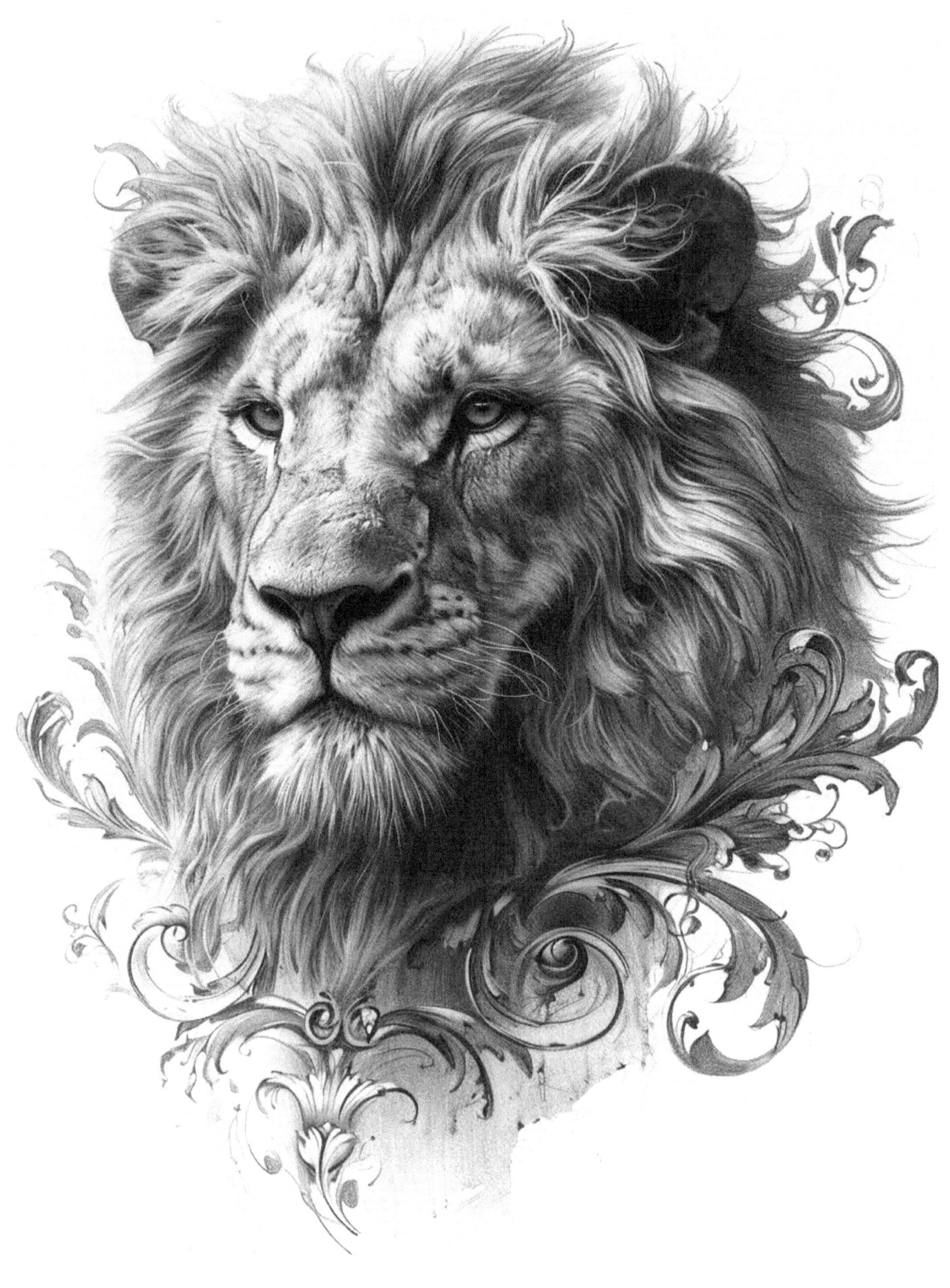

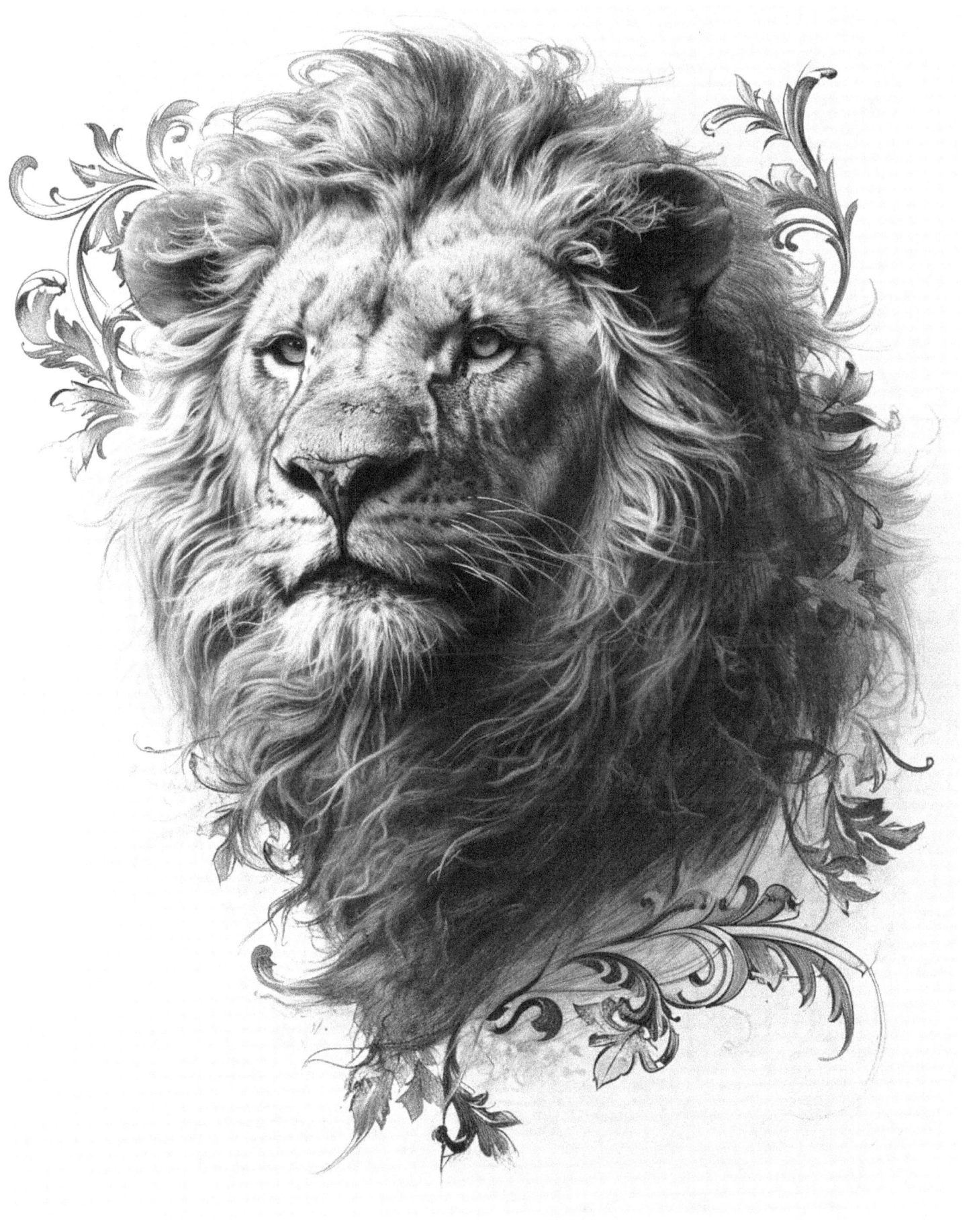

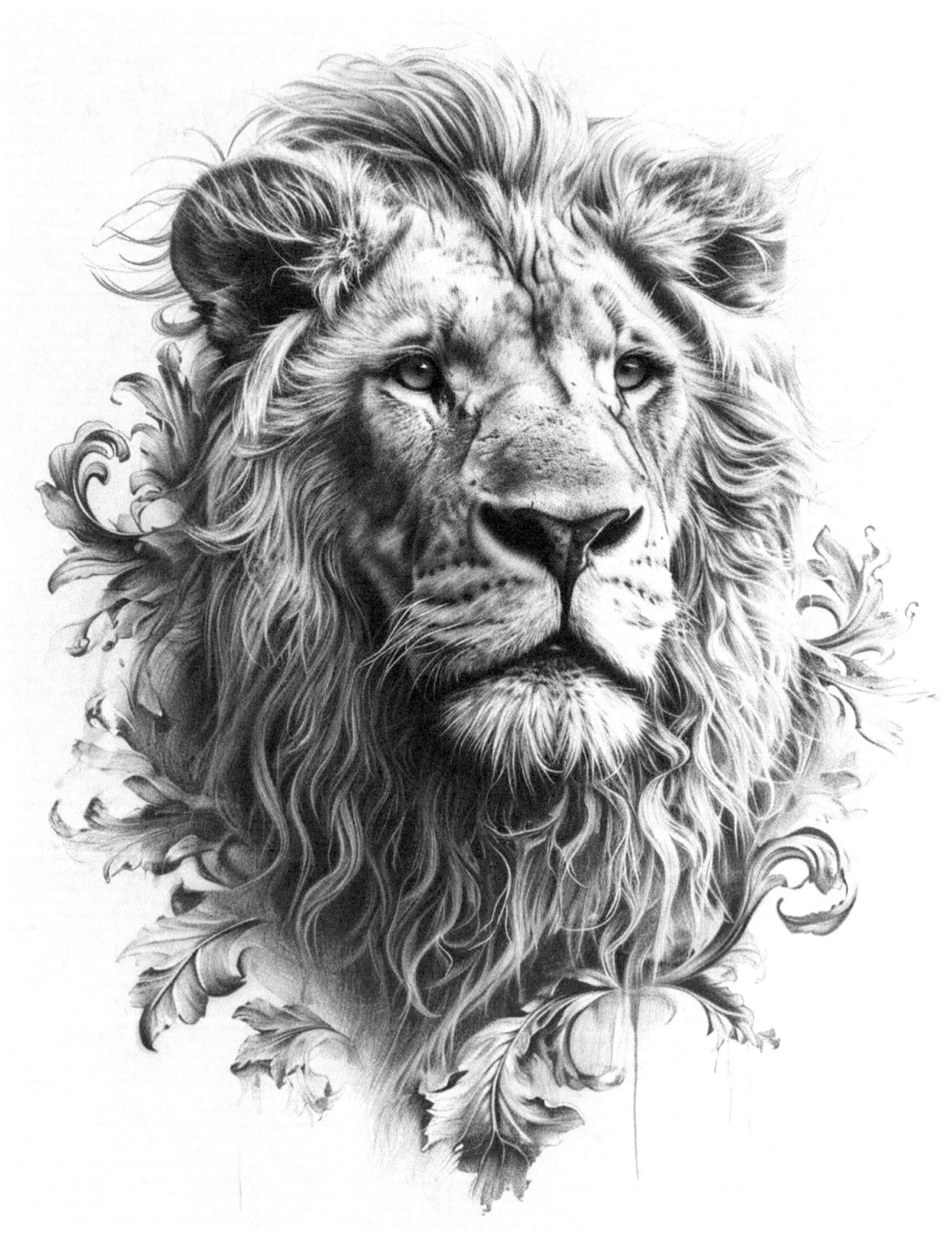

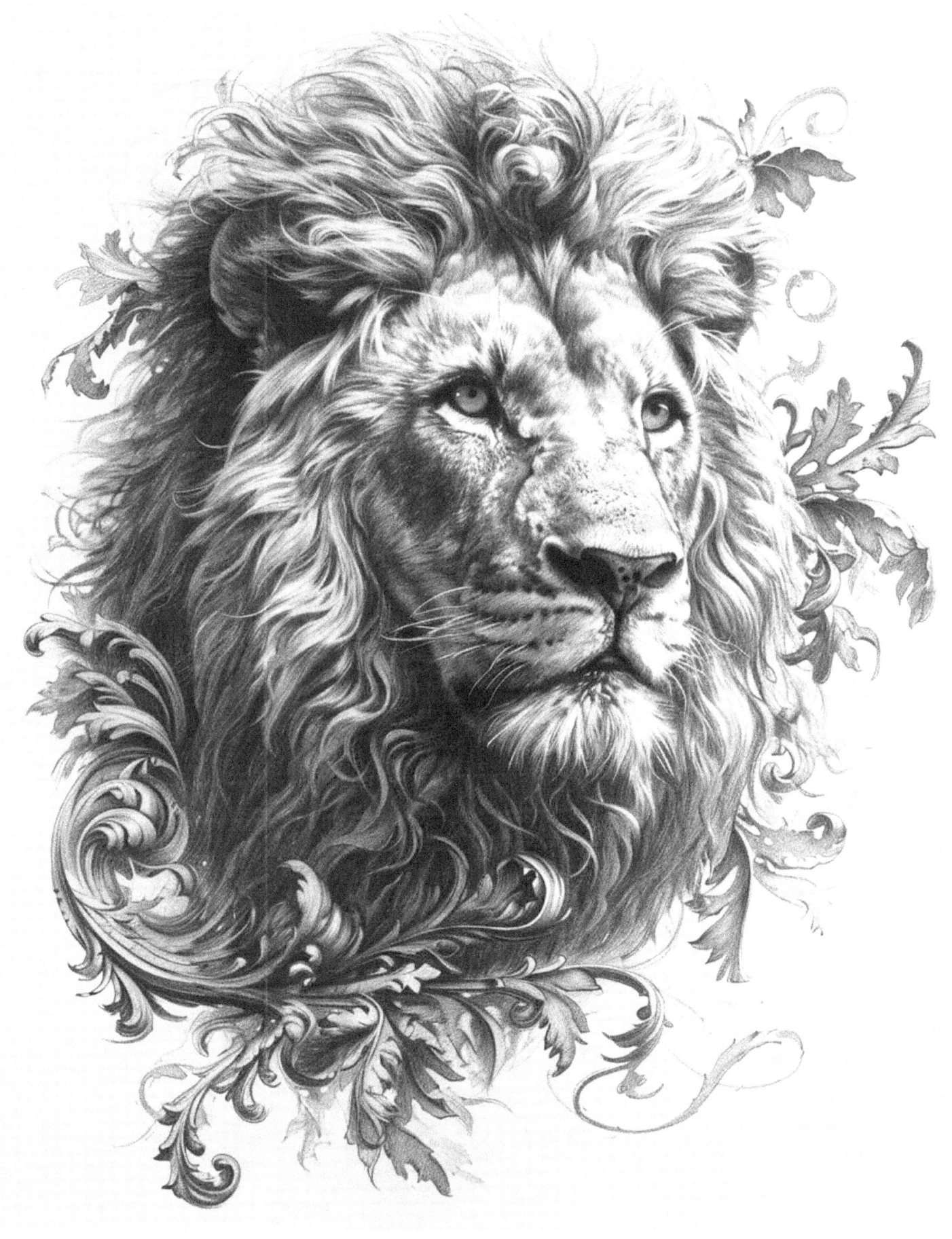

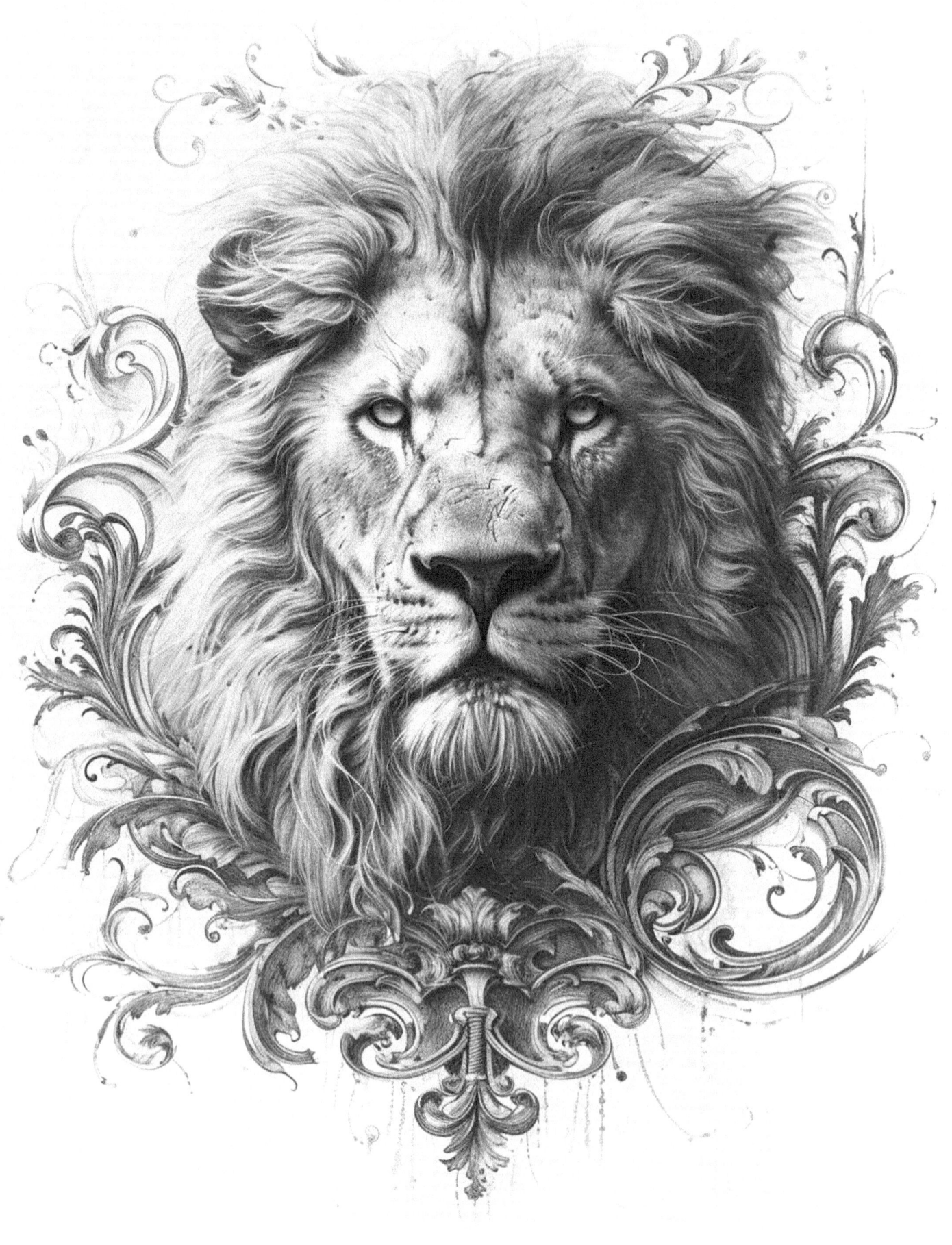

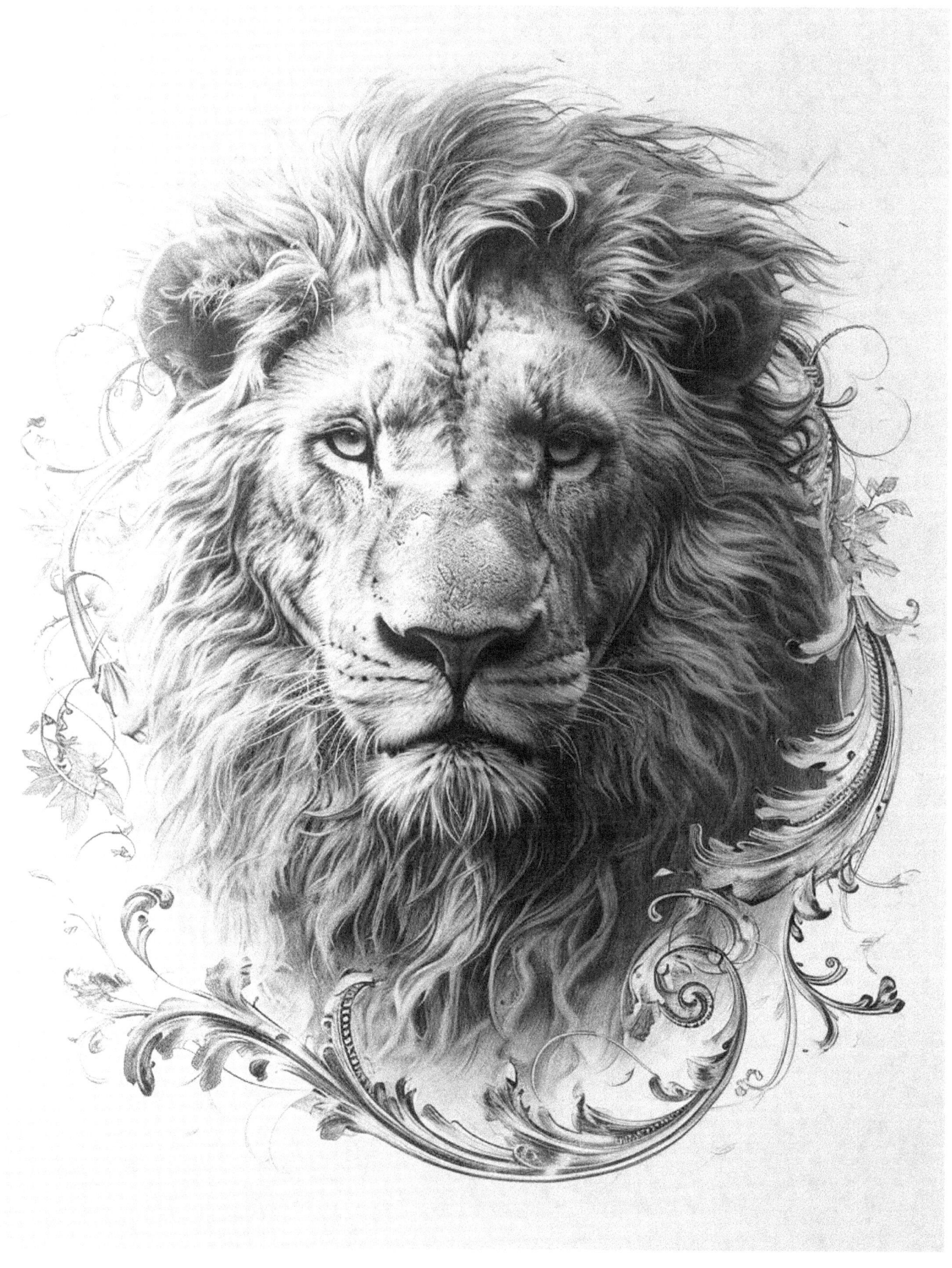

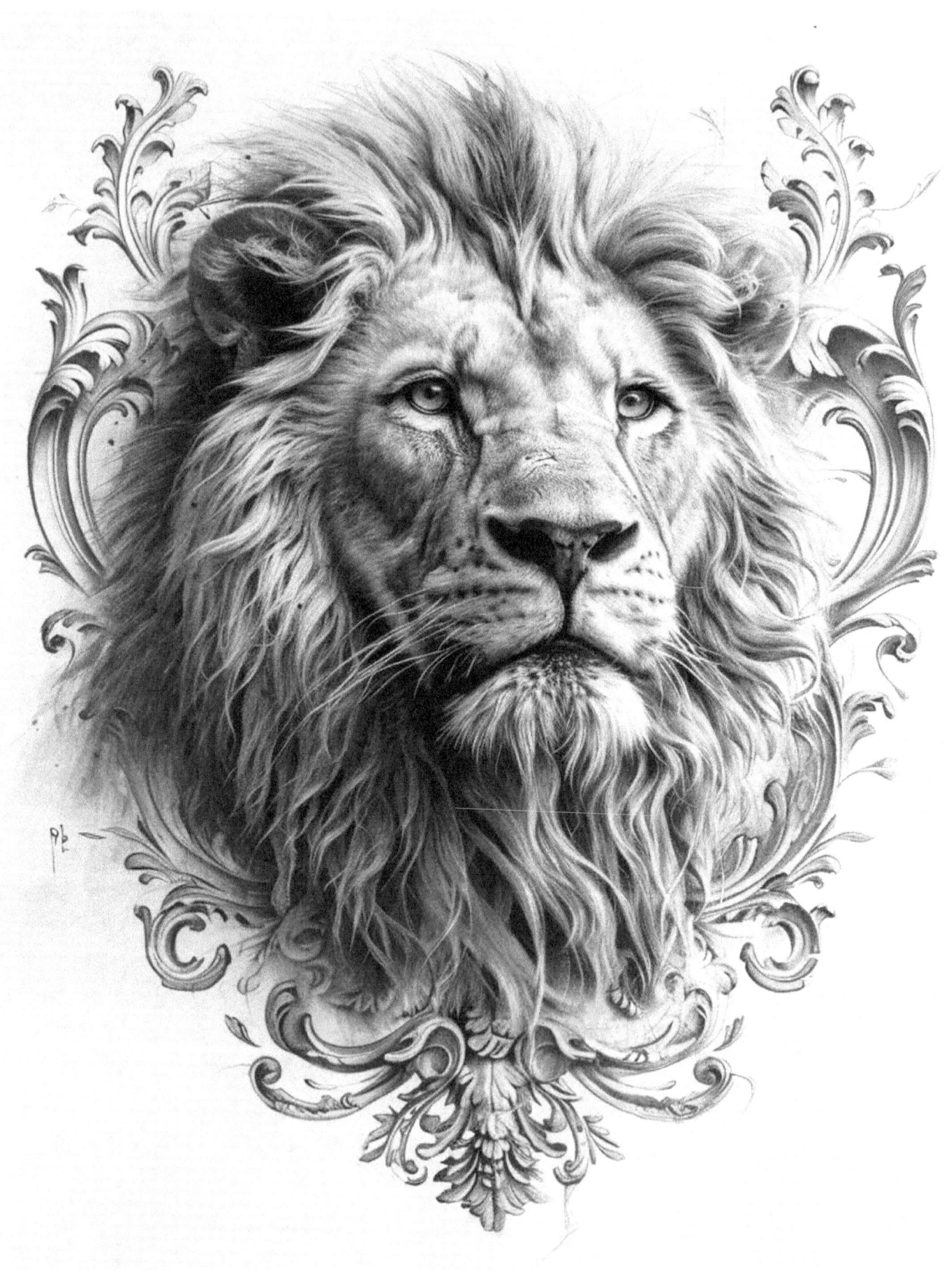

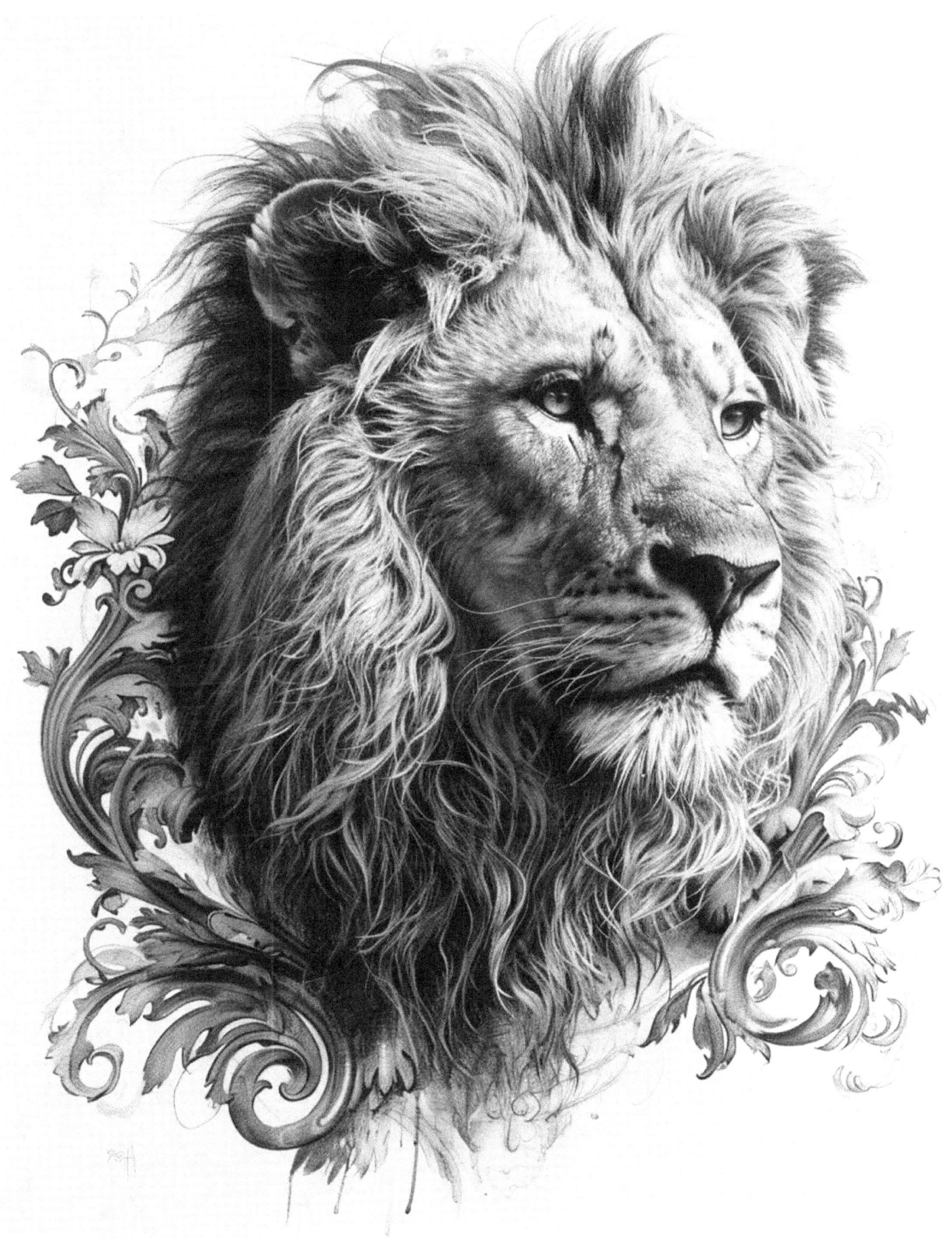

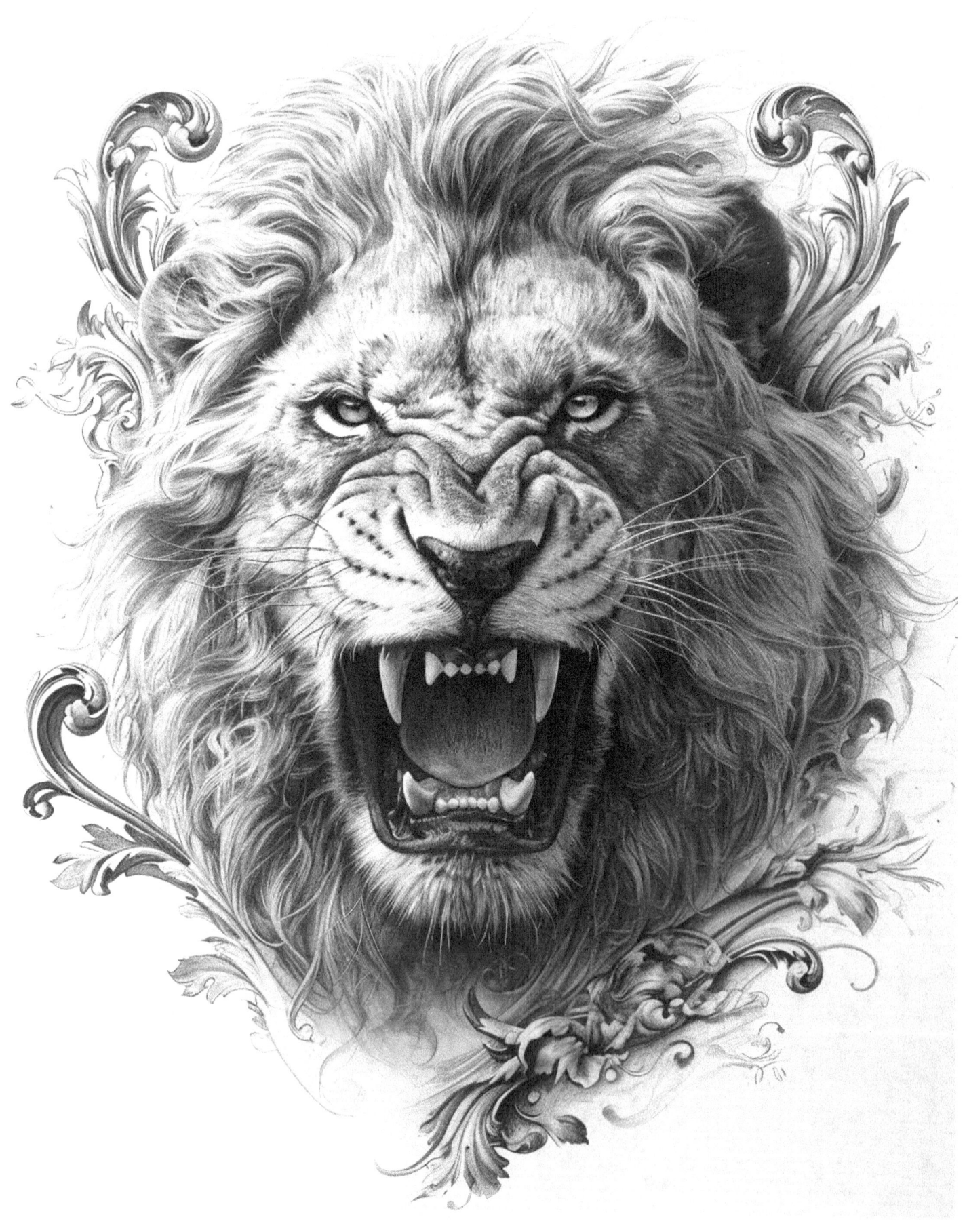

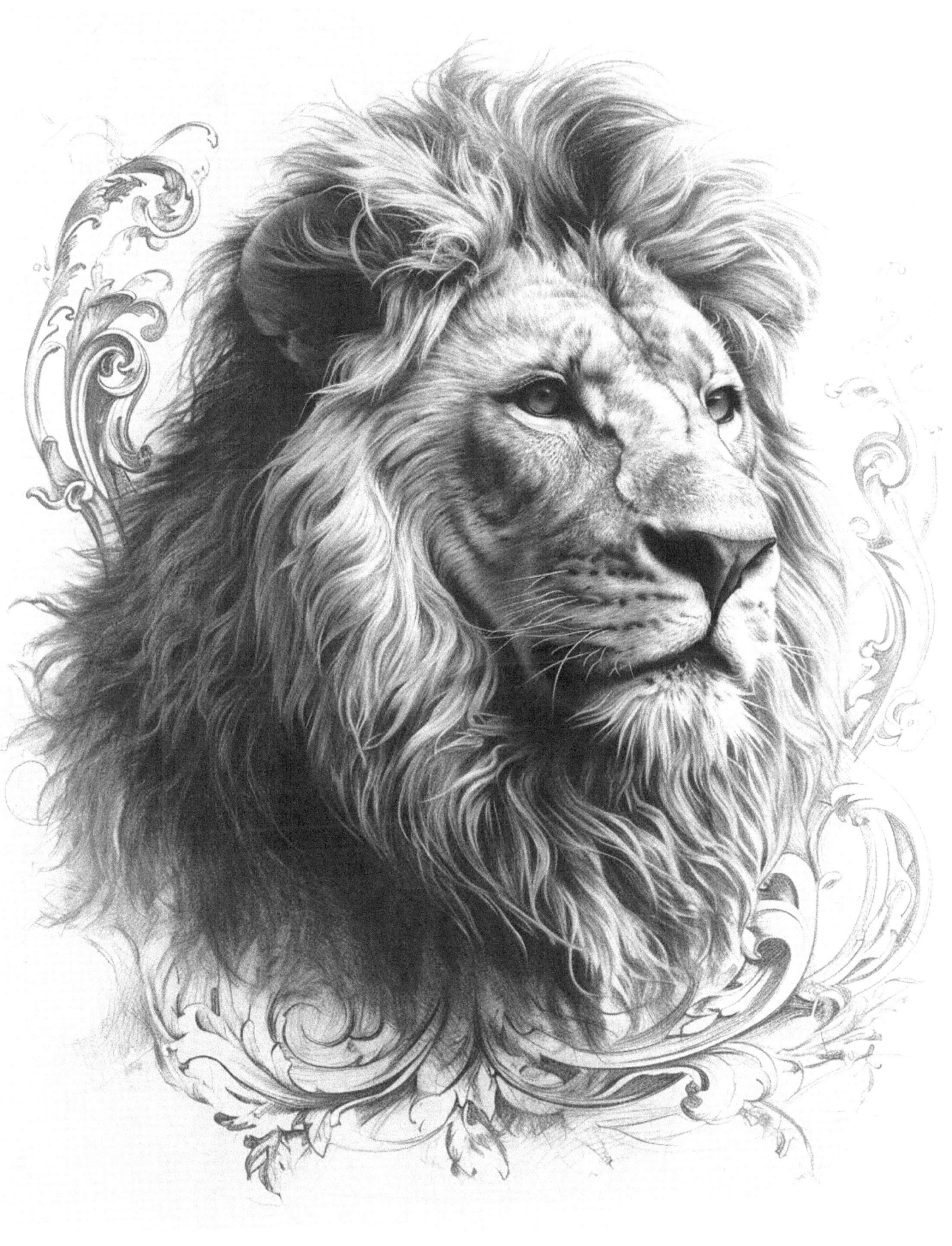

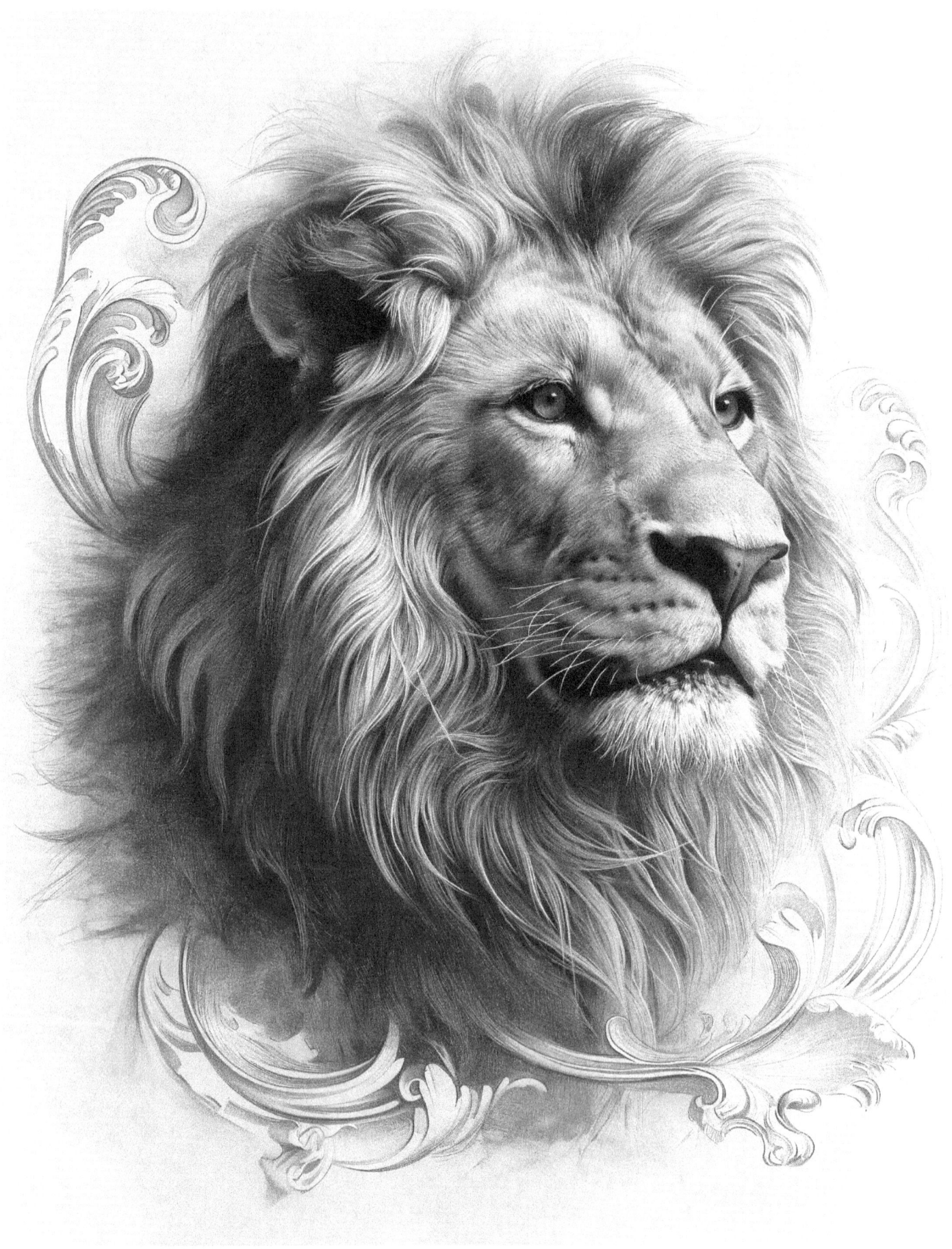

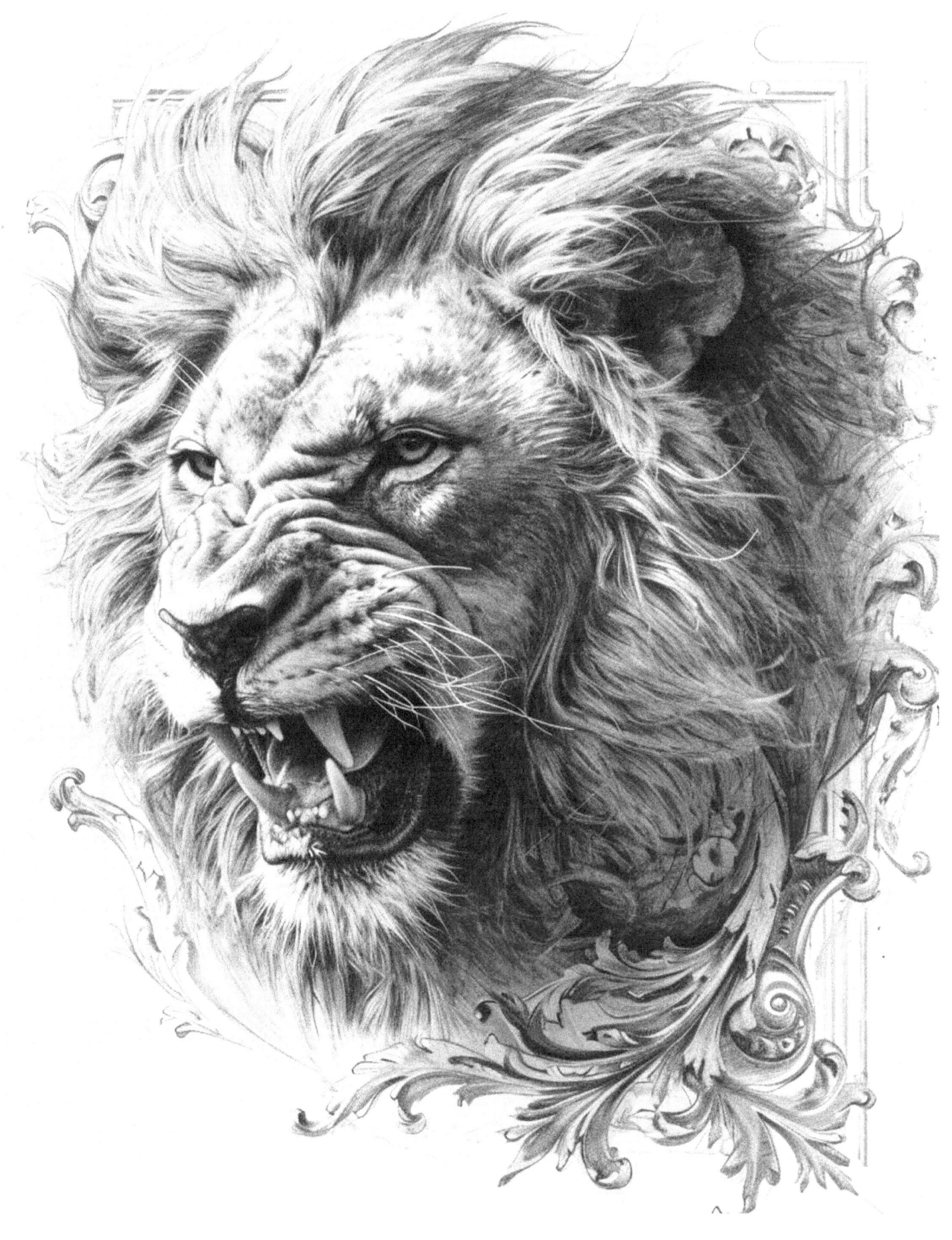

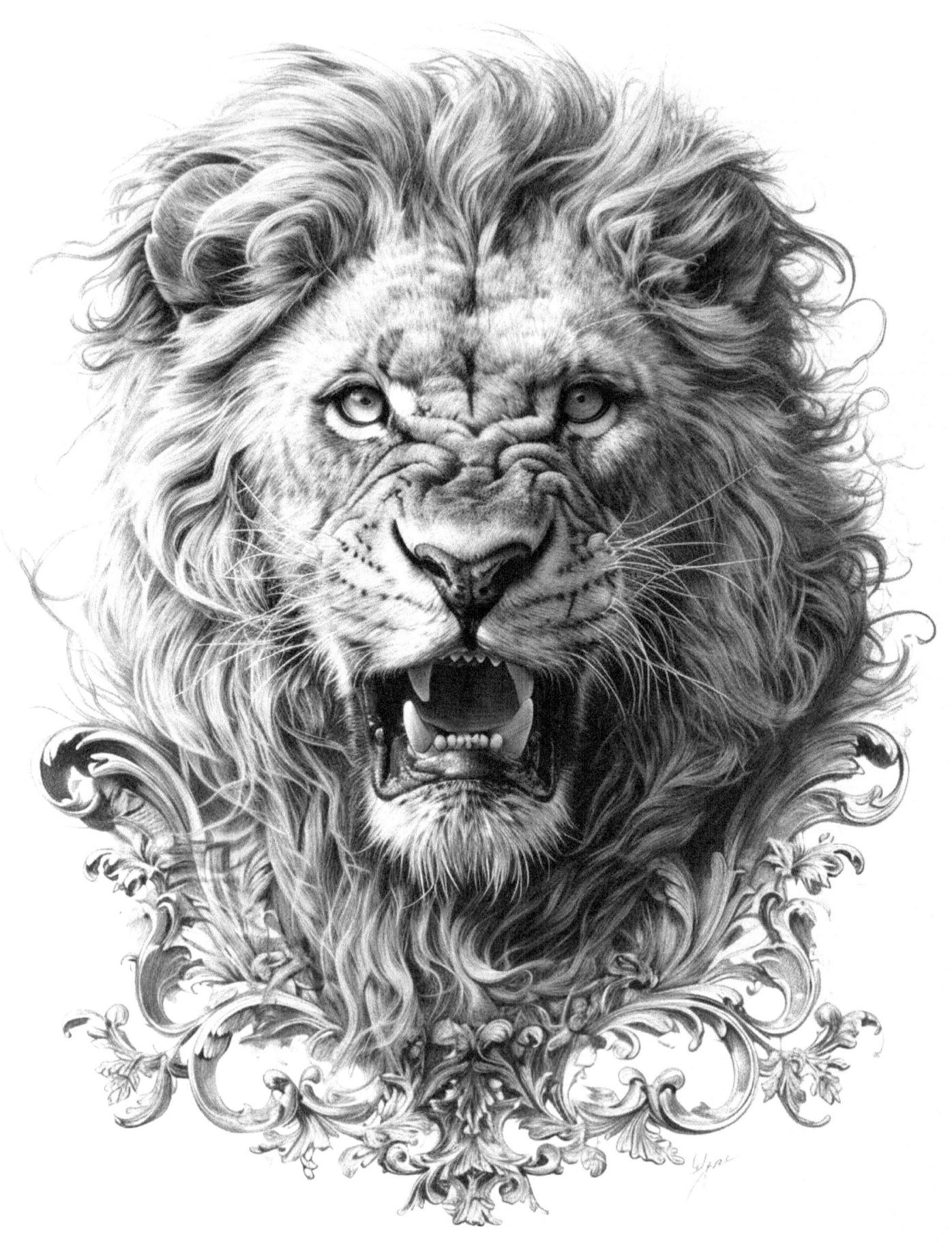

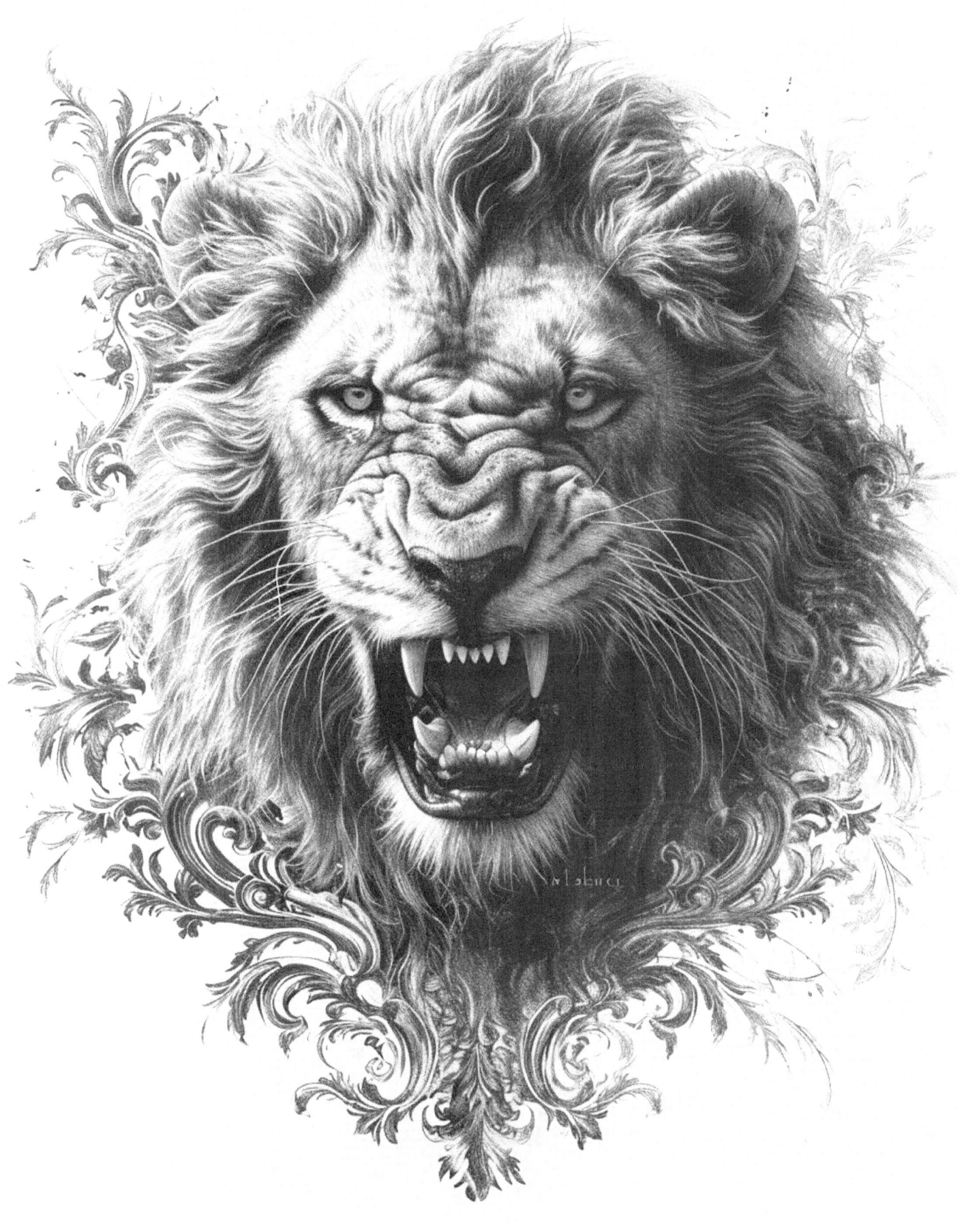

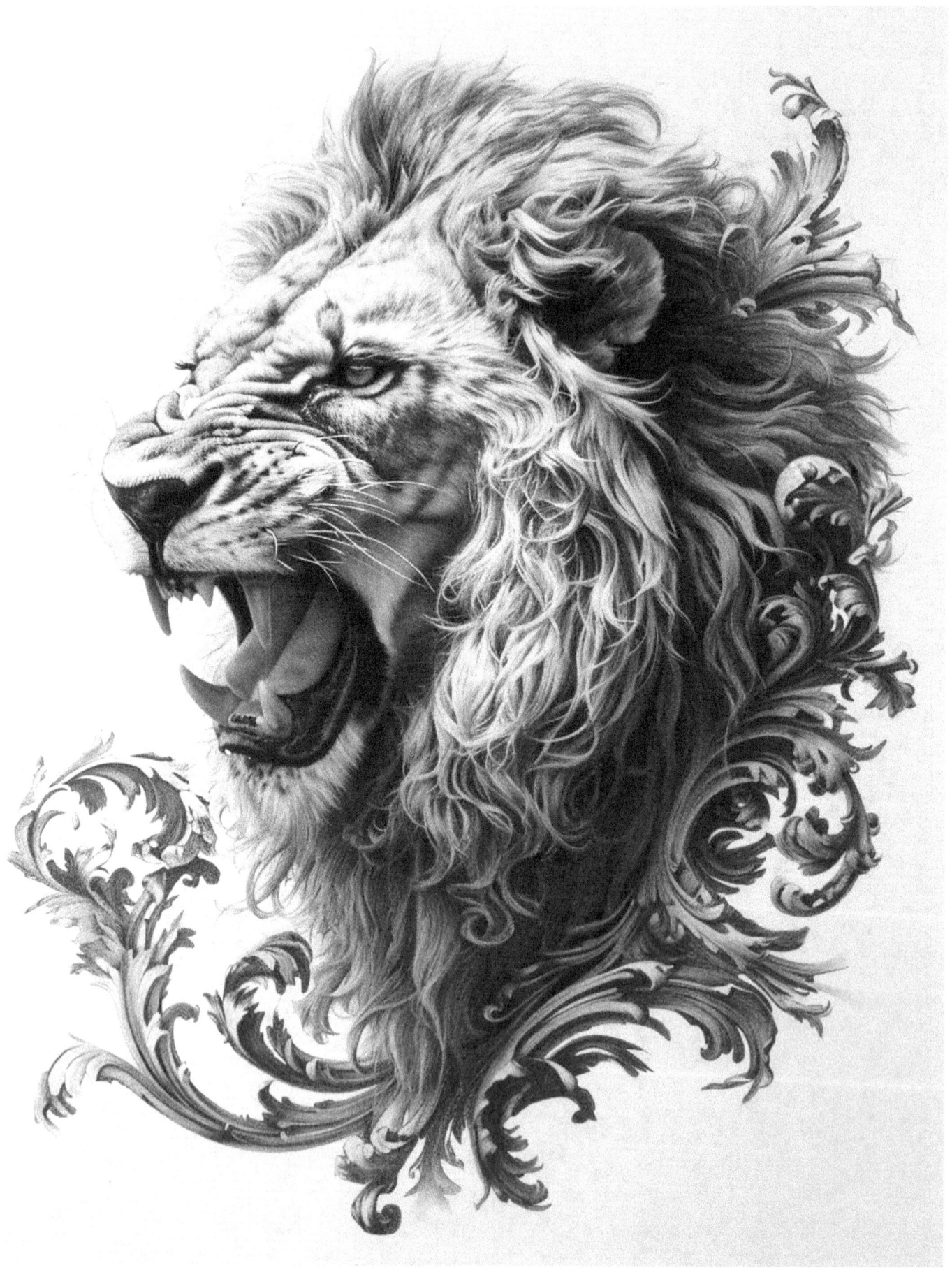

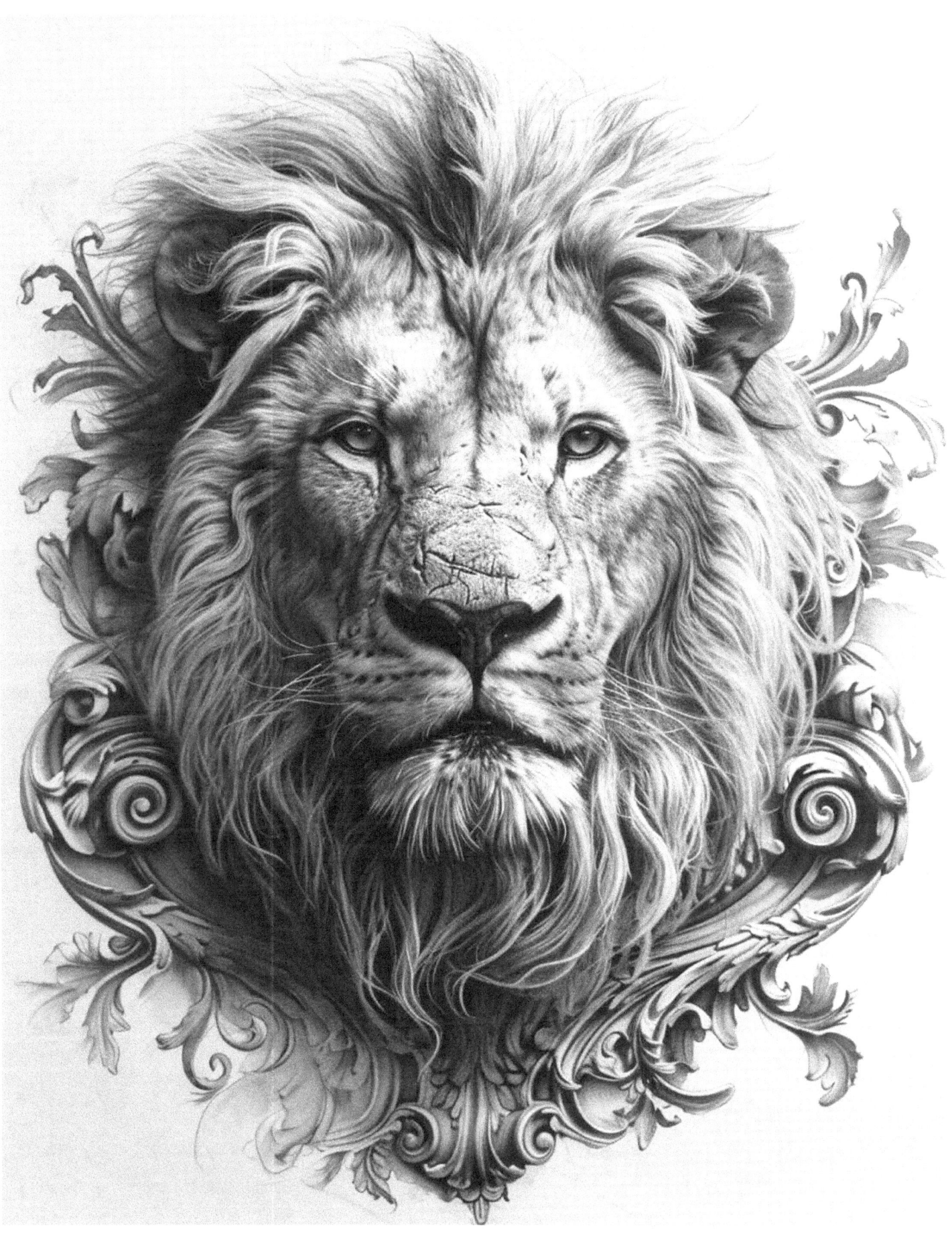

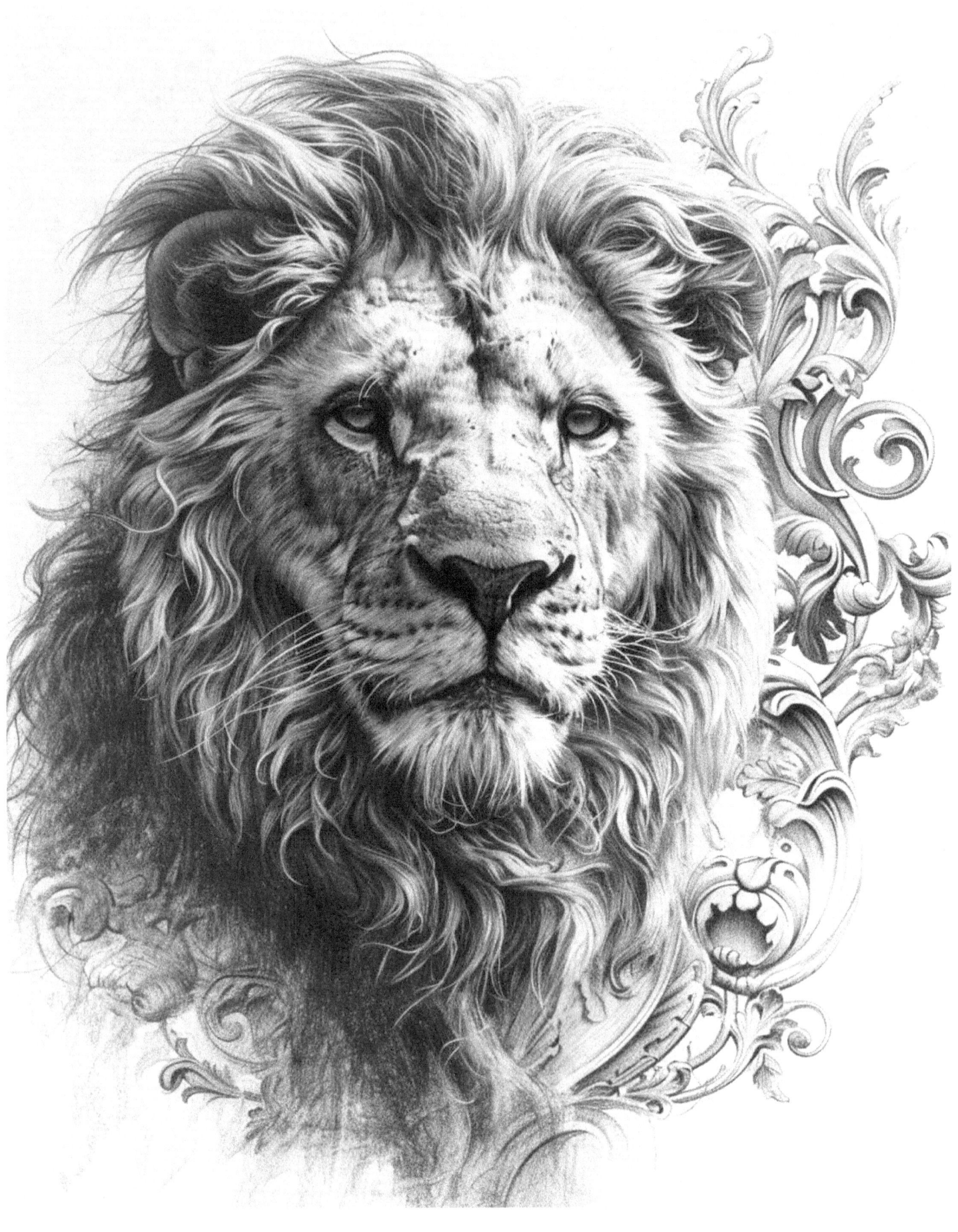

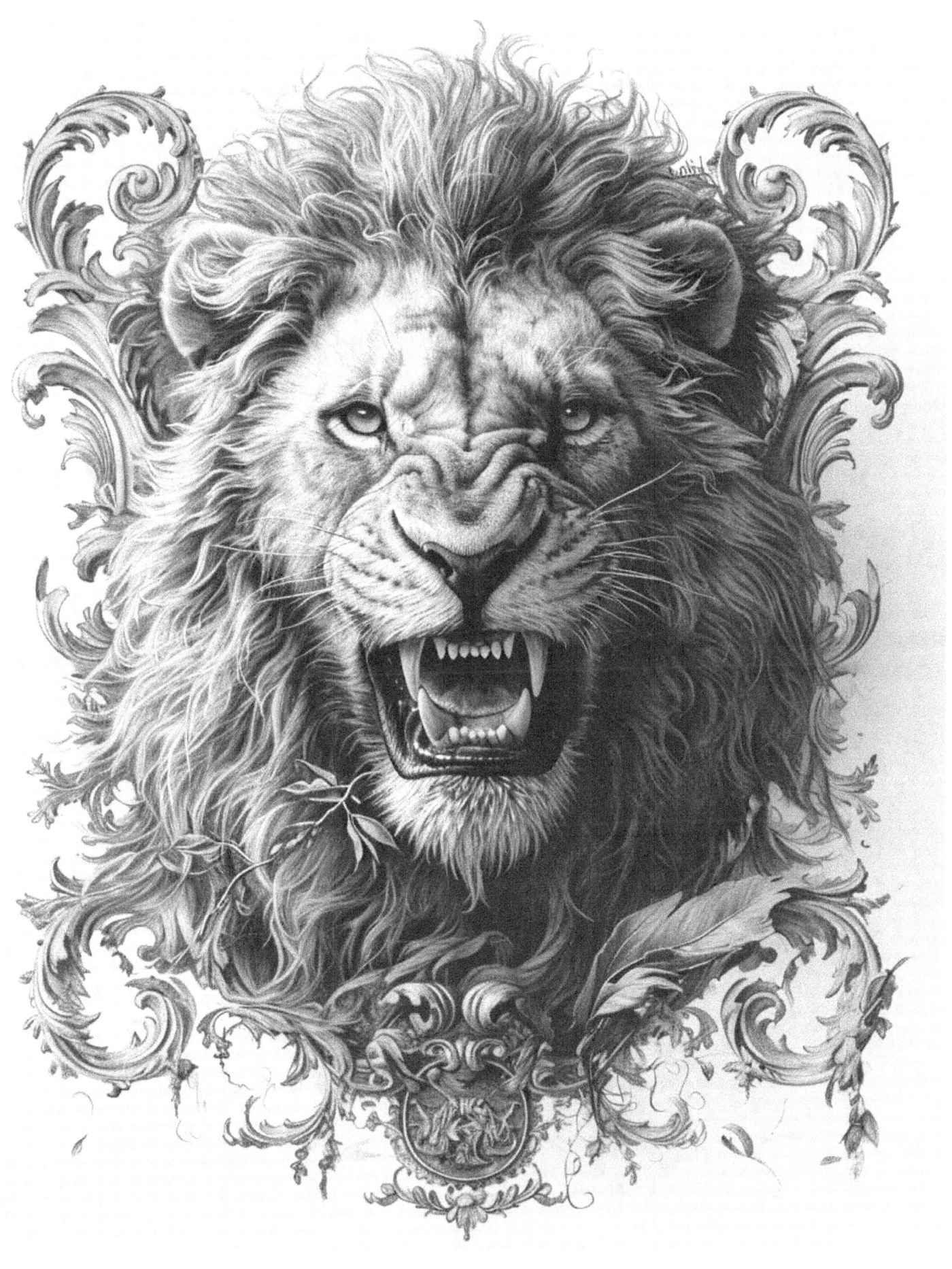

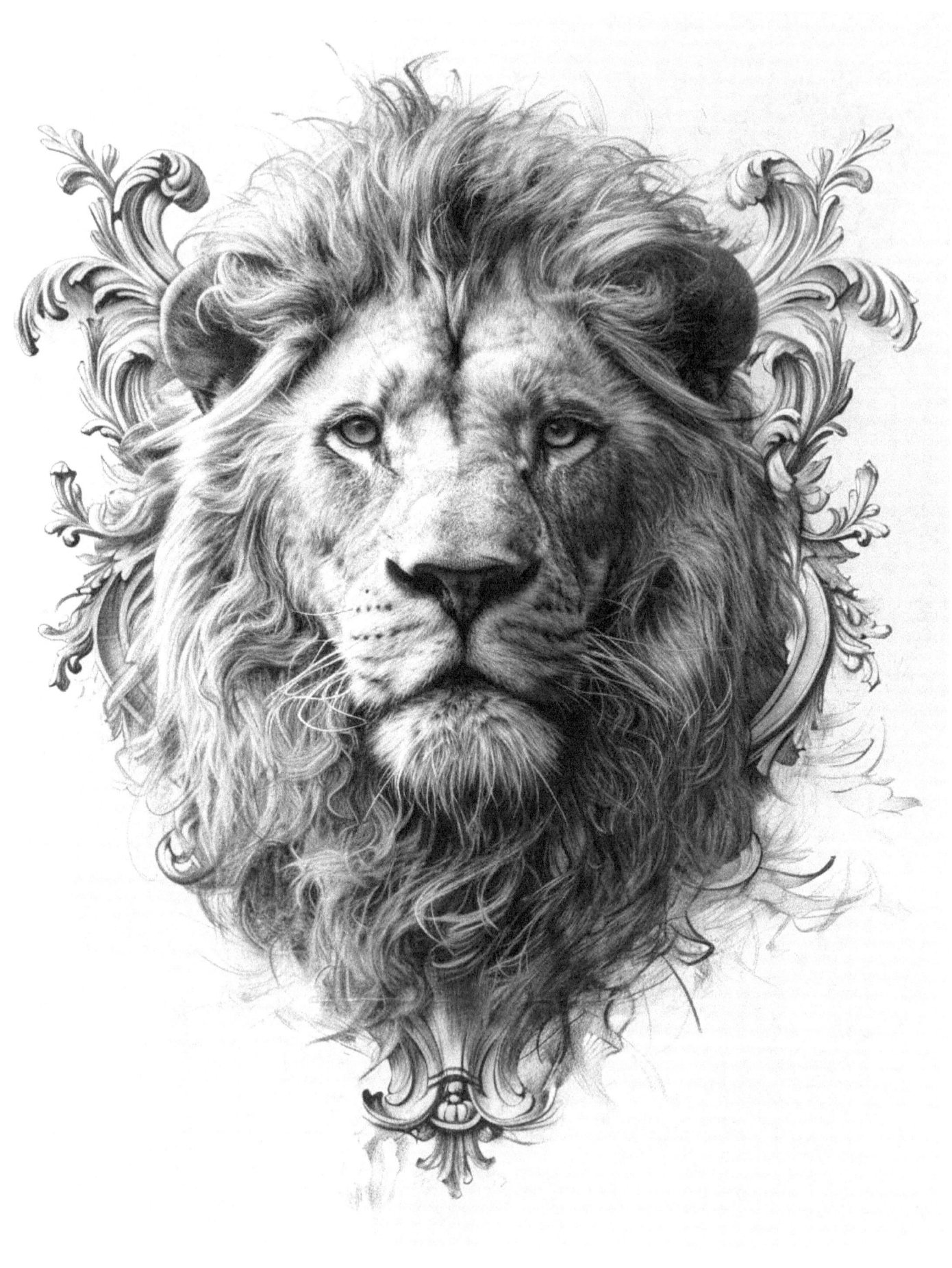

ABOUT THE AUTHOR

Immerse yourself in the captivating world of art, where imagination knows no bounds. With over three decades of experience as a painter, tattoo artist, and author, I have dedicated my life to the pursuit of artistic excellence.

Through countless hours of dedication, I have honed my skills in charcoal, pencils, and acrylic colors, specializing in the realms of realism, photorealism, and impressionism. My unique style blends elements of fantasy and impressionism, resulting in mesmerizing works of art that evoke deep emotions and leave a lasting impact.

In the realm of tattoo artistry, I have emerged as a trailblazer, revolutionizing the industry with my fresh and distinctive designs. Recognizing the need for innovation, I have created a new age of tattoo art that seamlessly combines my preferred style with eye-catching aesthetics. My designs not only captivate the eye but also empower individuals to express their individuality and uniqueness.

Expanding my creative horizons, I have delved into the world of coloring books. Gone are the days of simplistic designs with thick lines. I am on a mission to introduce the realms of realism and impressionism to the coloring book landscape. Each page of my coloring books offers intricate details and a chance for individuals to unleash their inner artist, resulting in remarkable and vibrant creations.

But my artistic endeavors don't stop there. I am currently engrossed in the creation of photo reference books that showcase wildlife and nature in unprecedented ways. These books will transport you to a world of vivid colors, breathtaking imagery, and seemingly impossible poses.

Prepare to be captivated by the untamed beauty of the natural world, brought to life through my keen eye for detail and my passion for pushing artistic boundaries.

Join me on an awe-inspiring journey where creativity knows no limits. Together, let's explore new dimensions of artistry, where fresh perspectives, remarkable designs, and boundless inspiration await.

Welcome to my world of art, where dreams become reality, and the extraordinary is transformed into tangible beauty

Scan the QR code below in order to download the PDF.

You will need WINRAR (or equivelant program)
to open the archive. Enter the password :

LionsRoyalResource2!

If download does not work please contact us at our Facebook page
https://www.facebook.com/DivineTattooDesign/

Follow us on facebook   Subscribe me at YouTube   My Books on Amazon
                                                                  SCAN ME

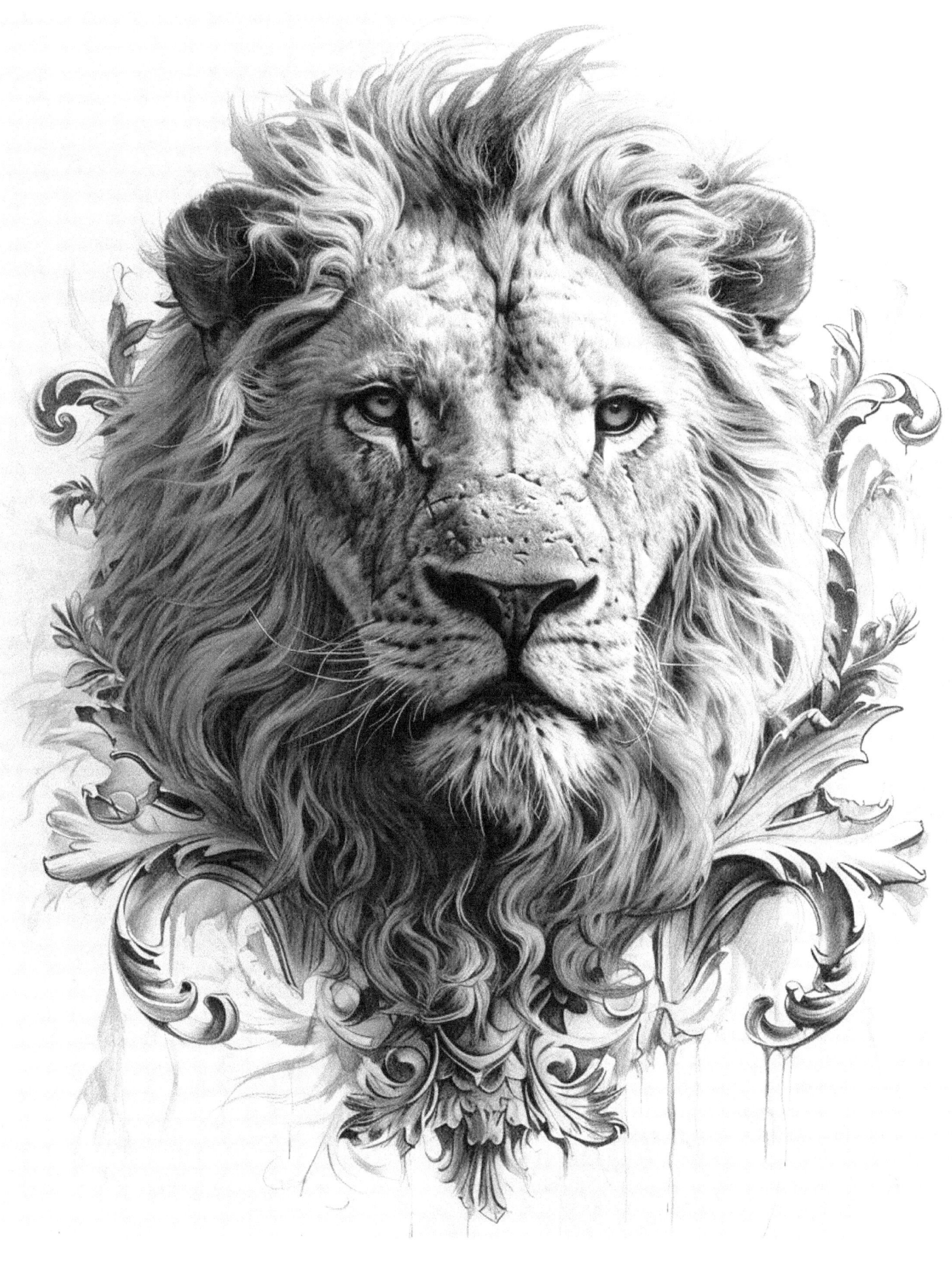

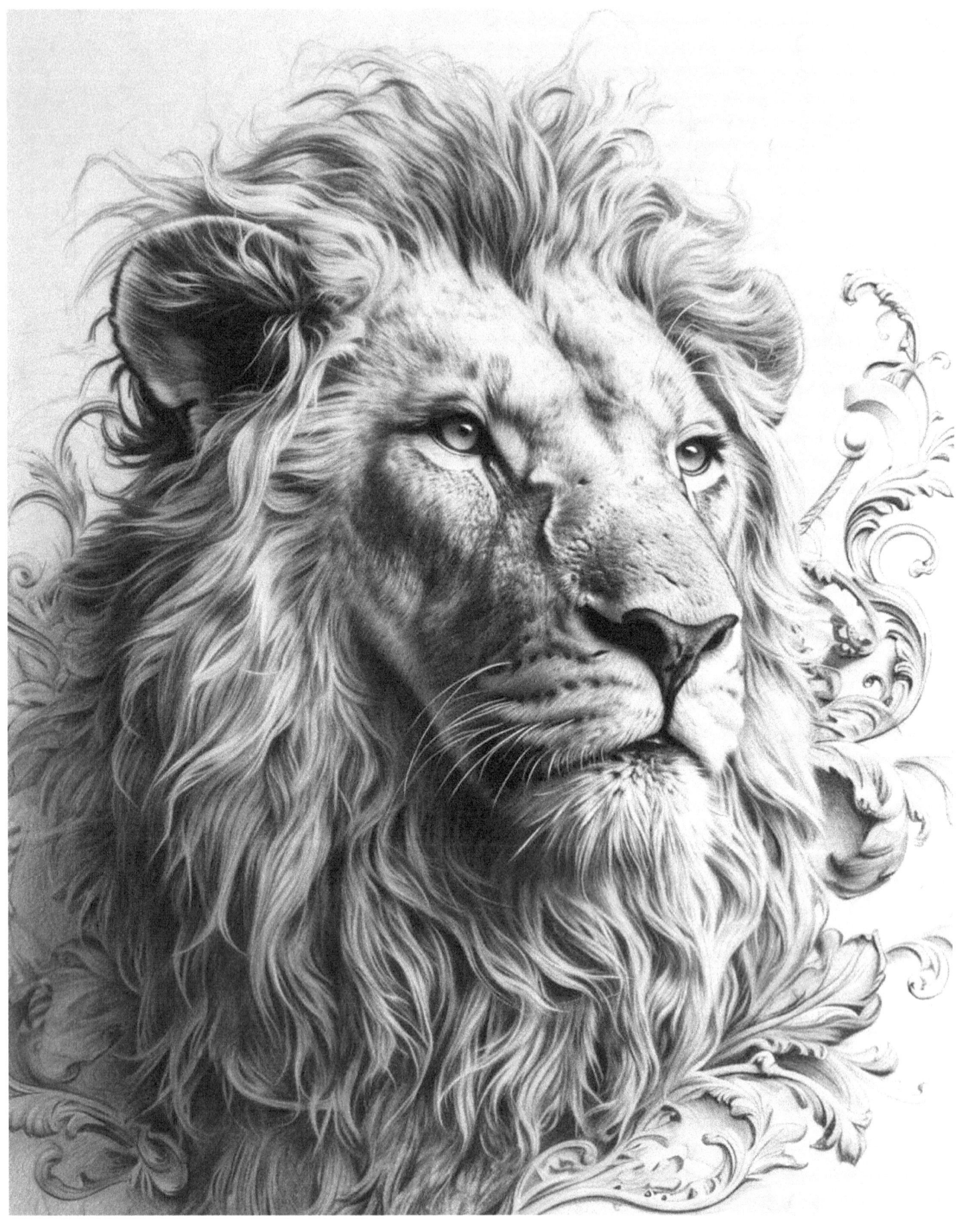

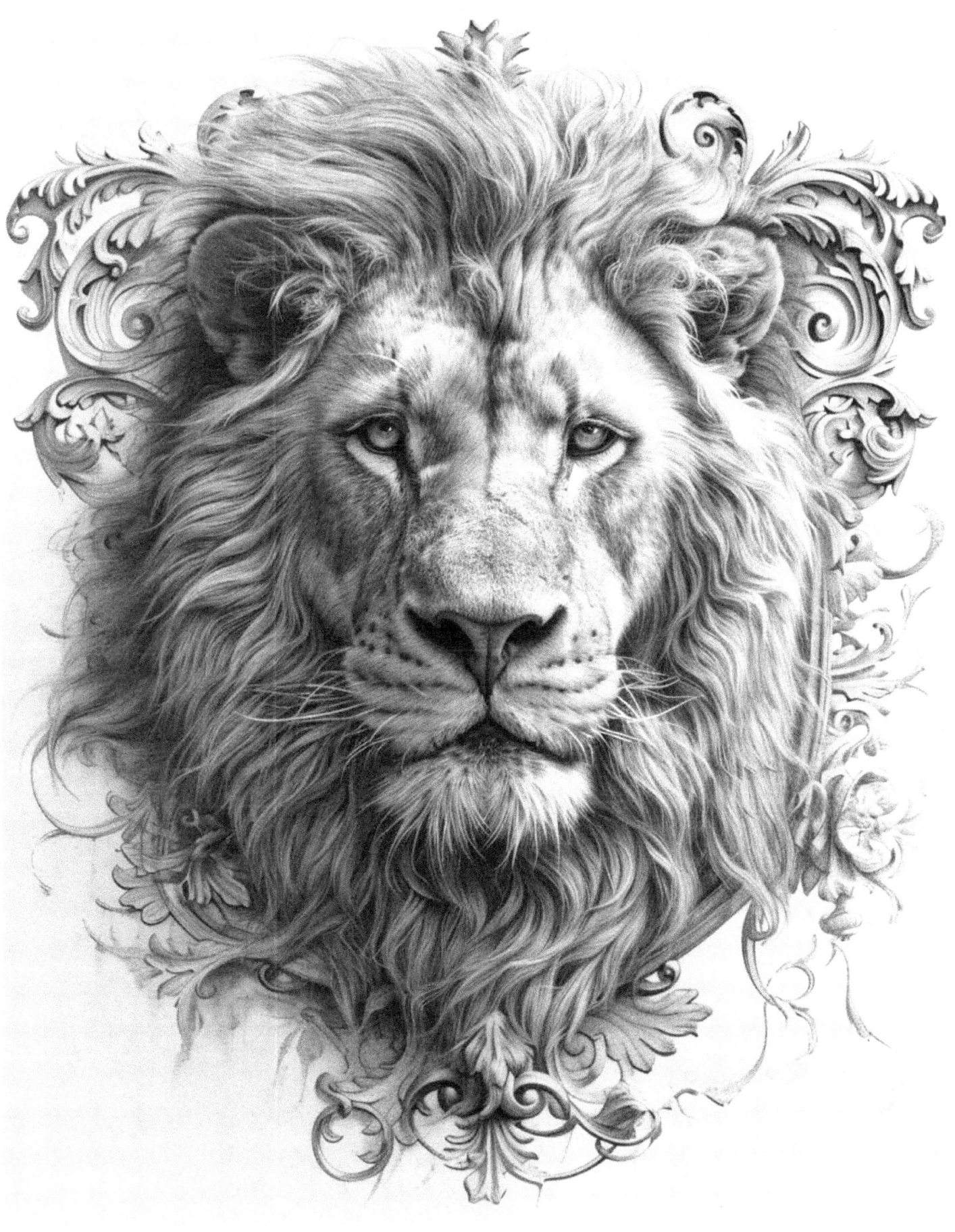

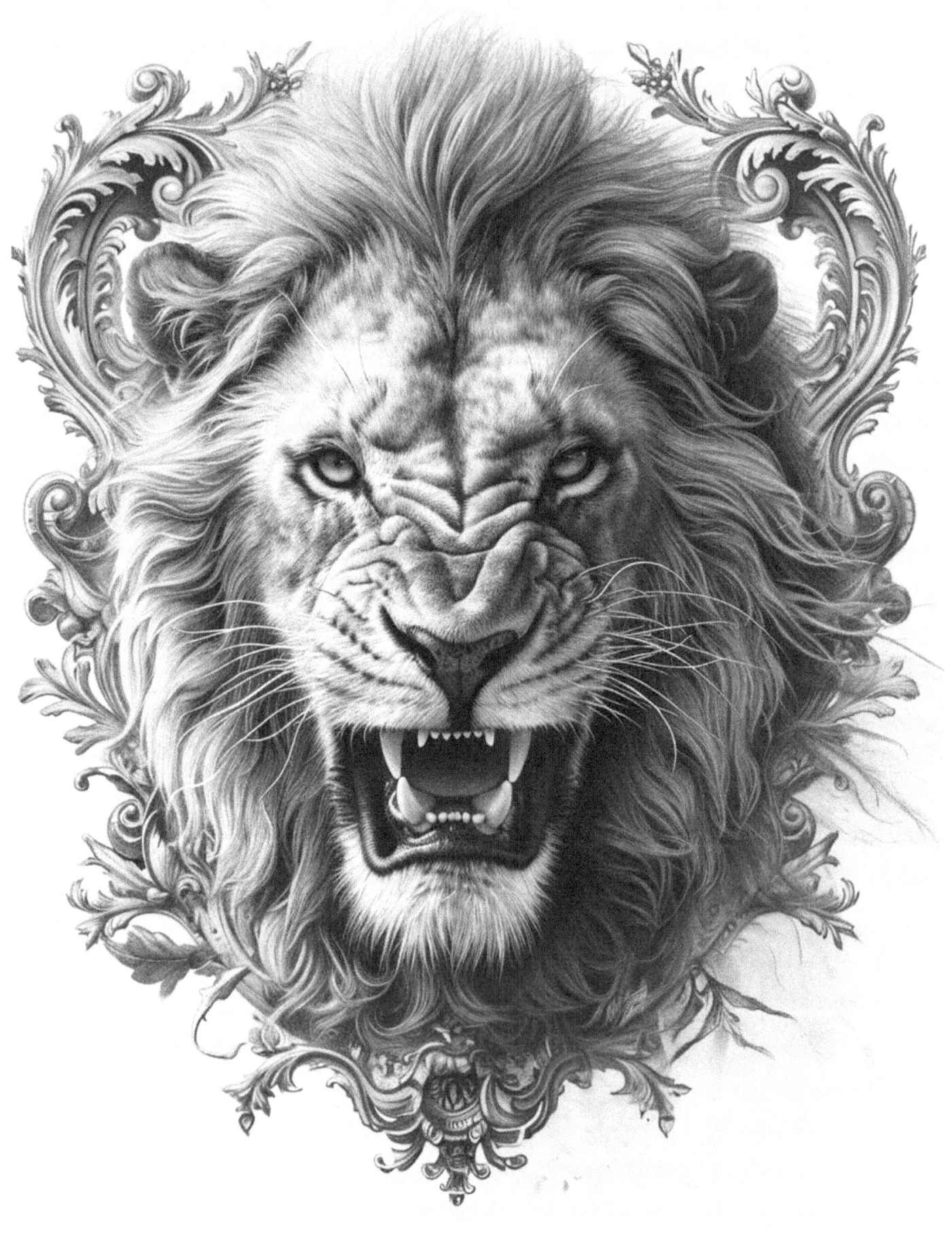

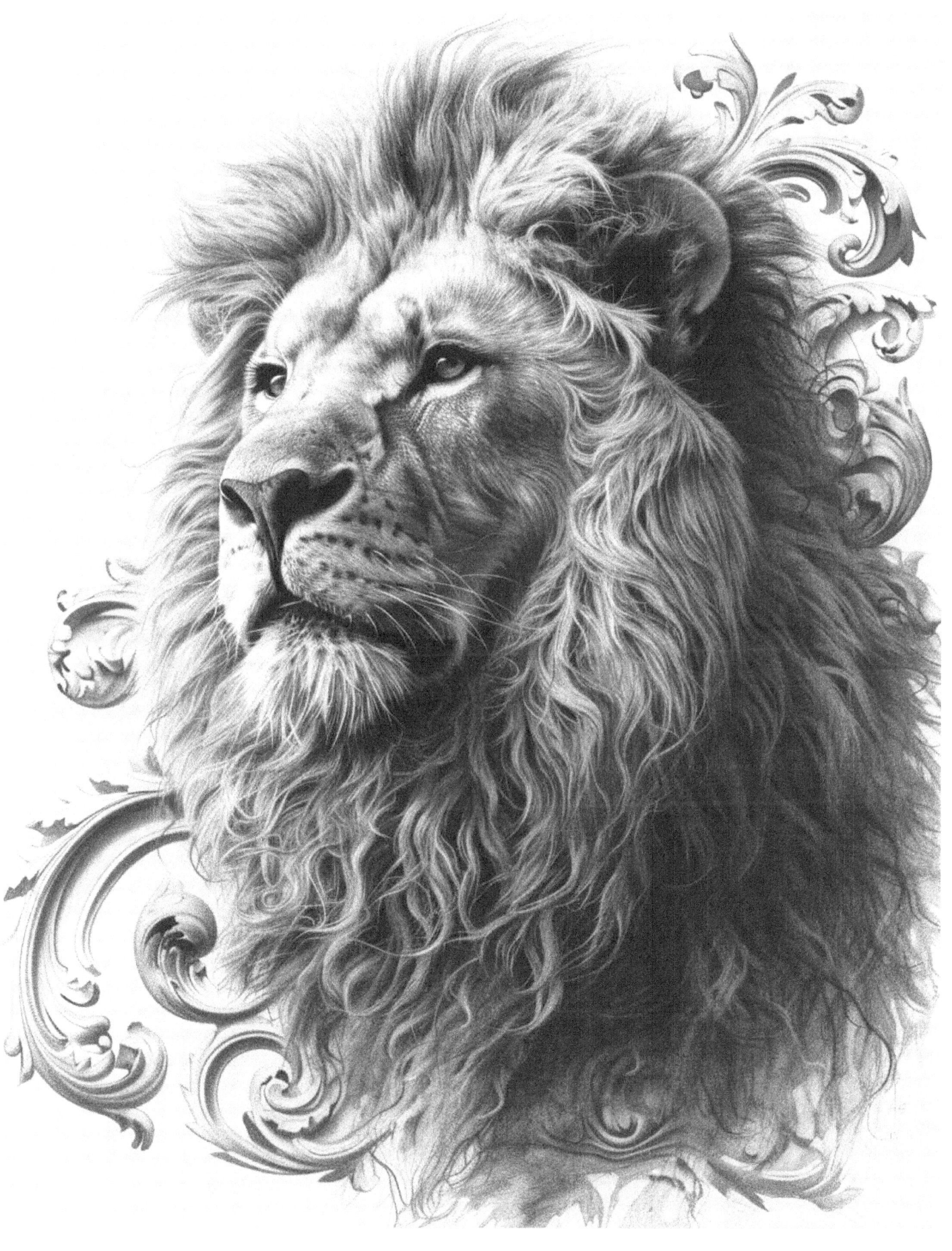

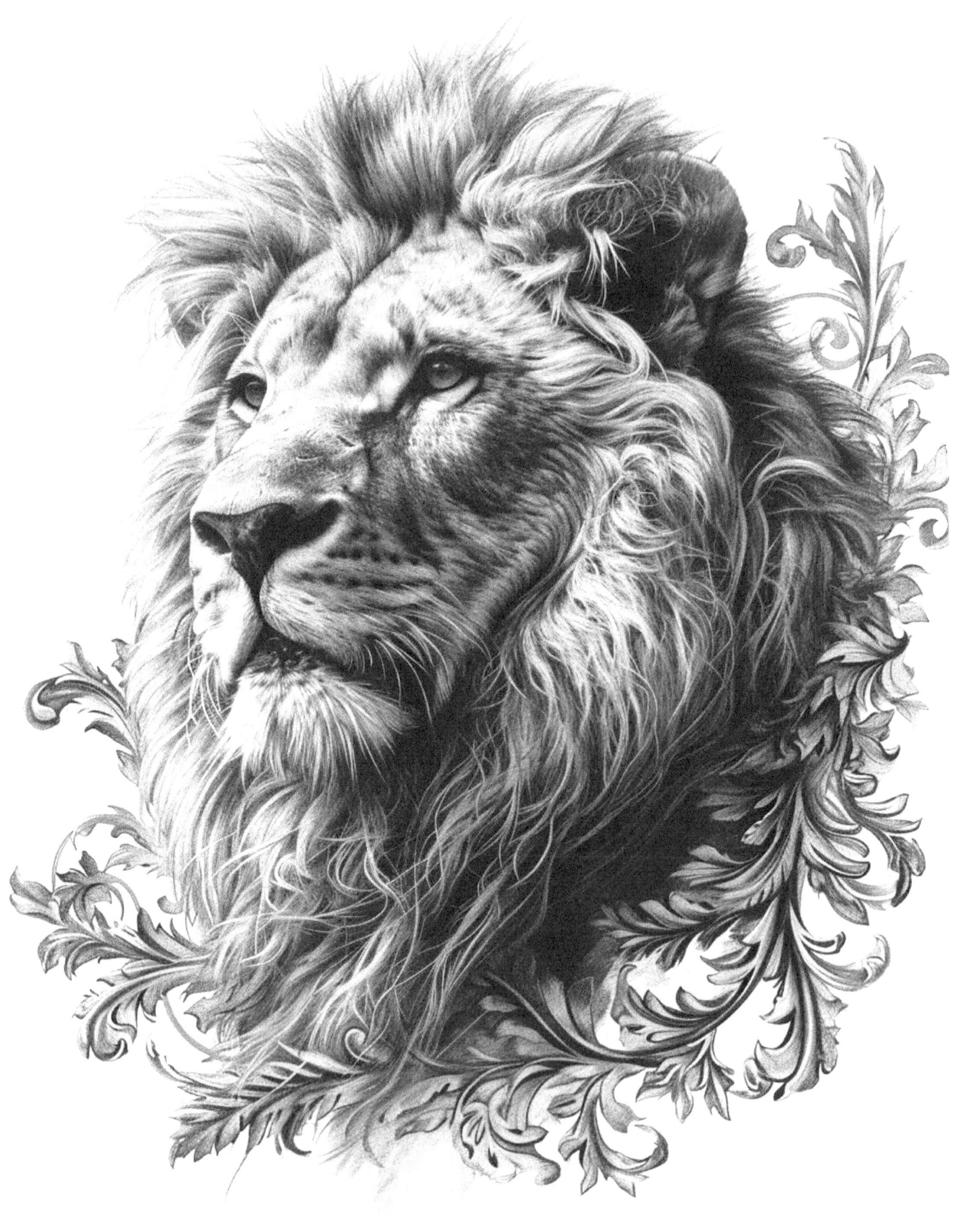

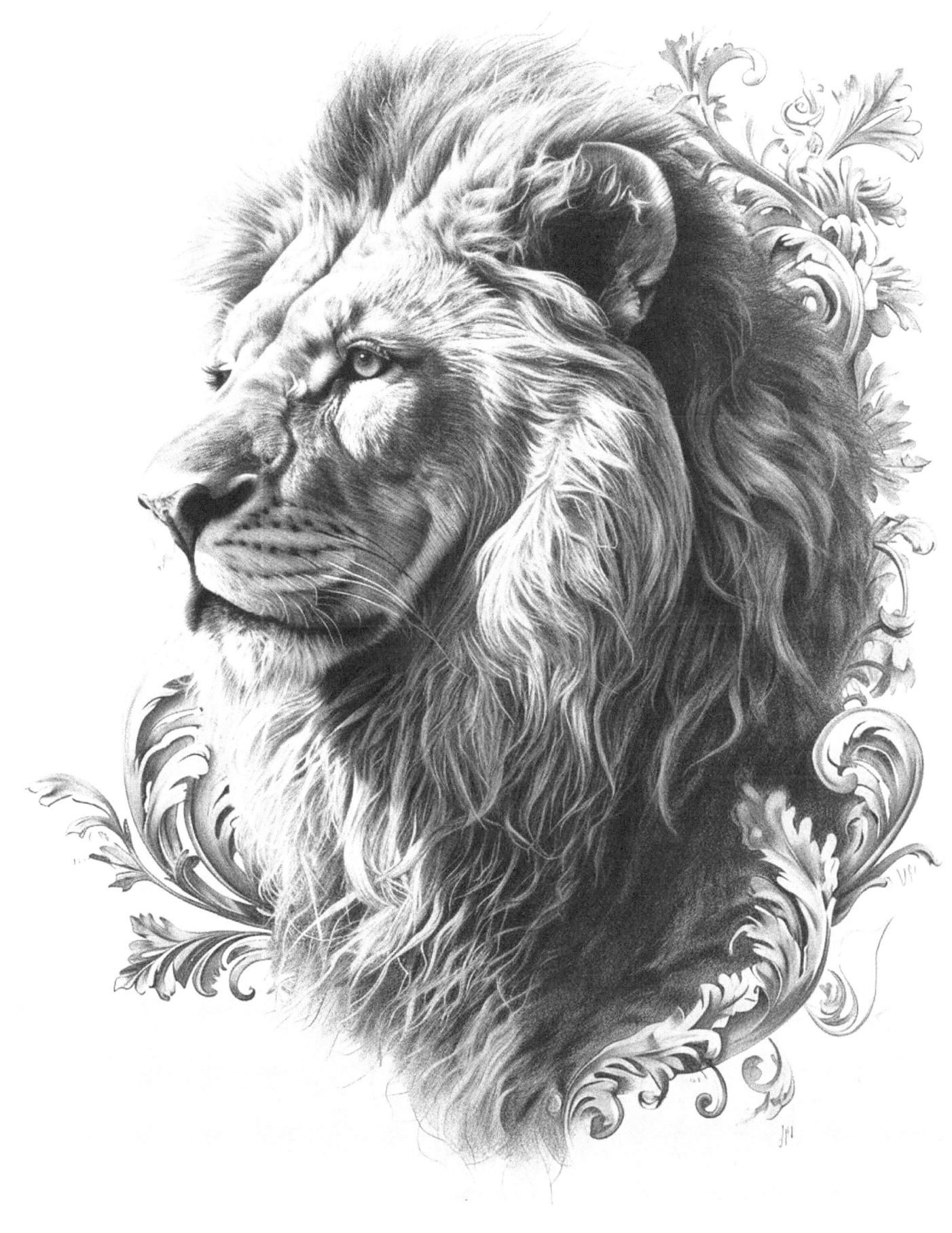

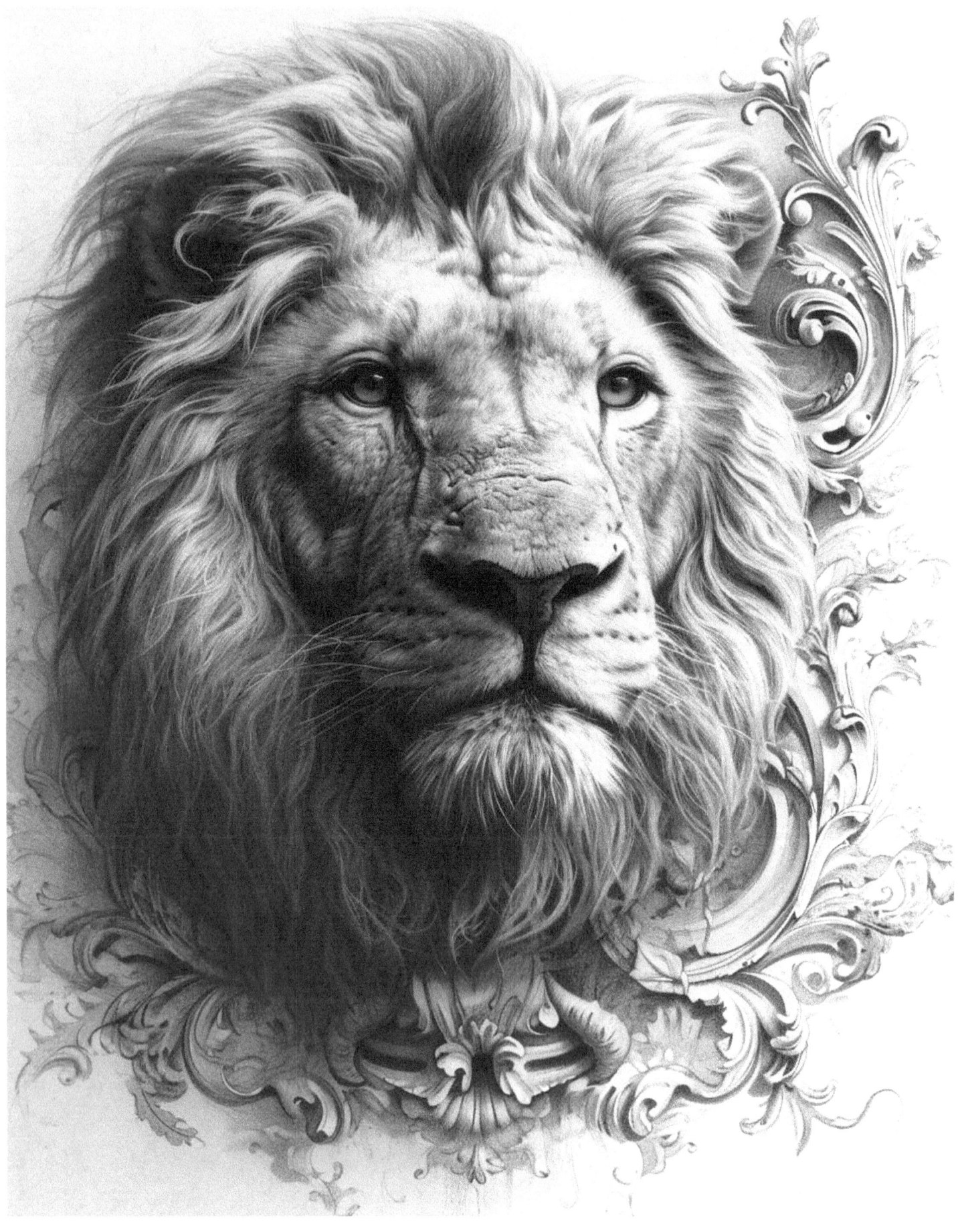

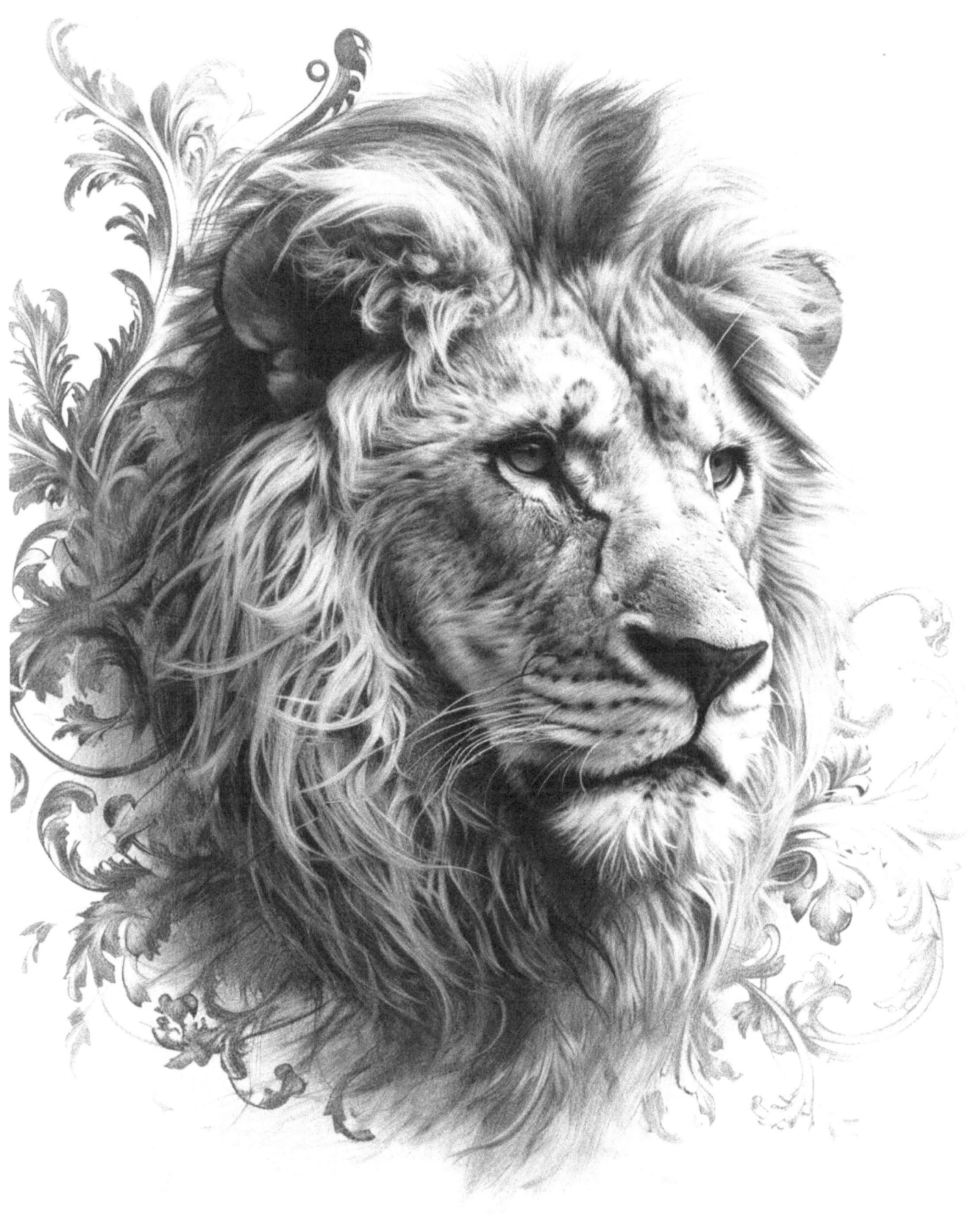

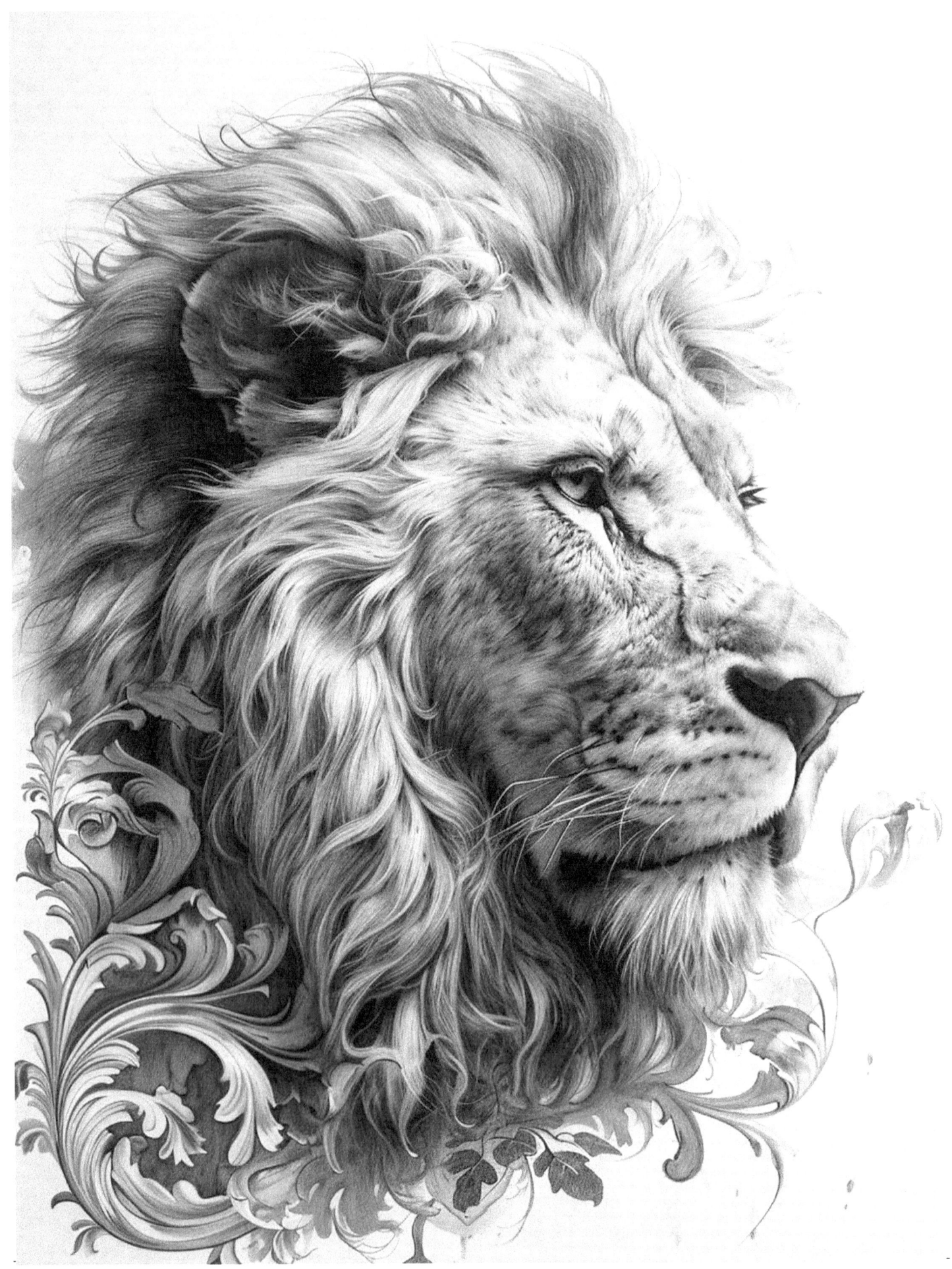

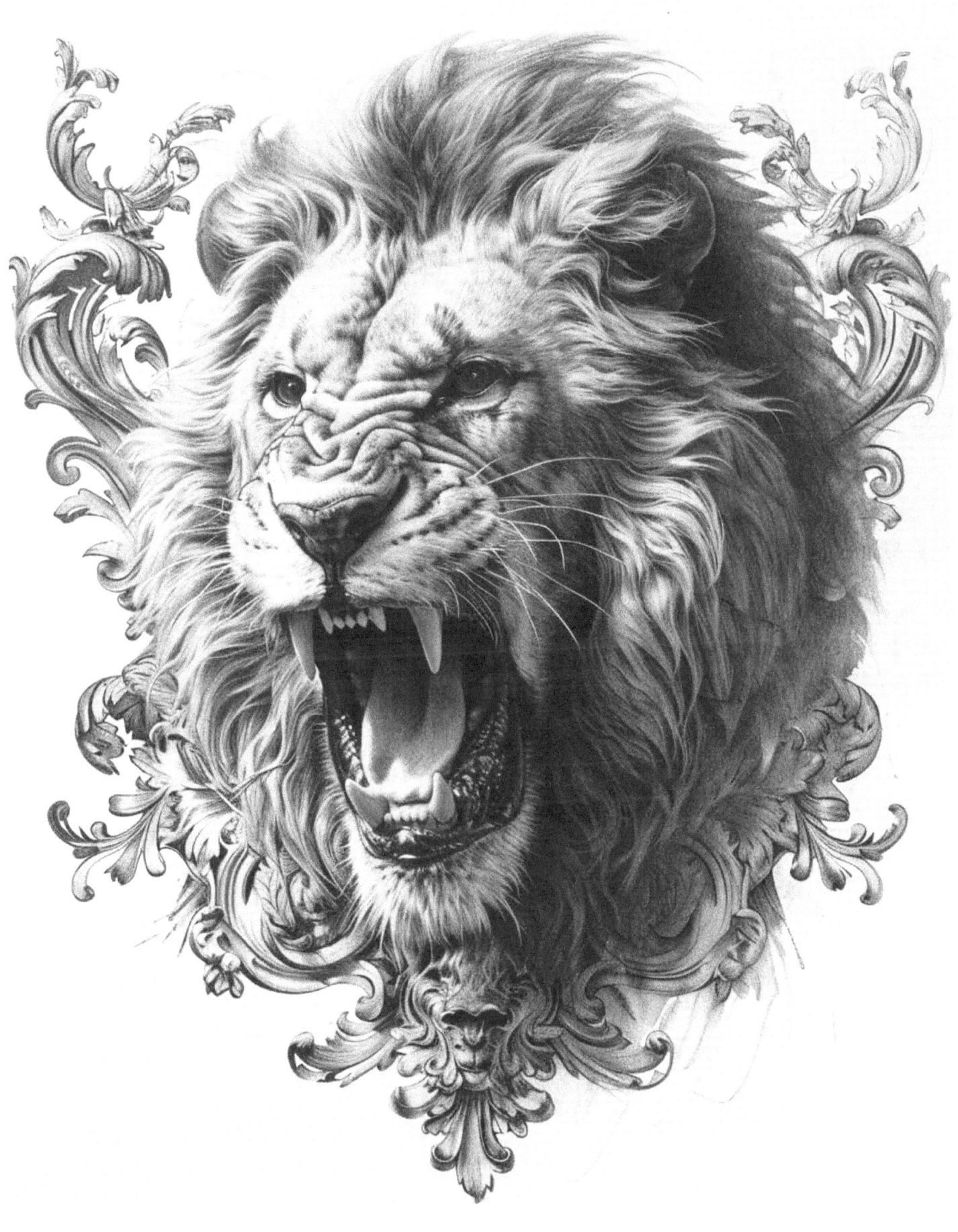

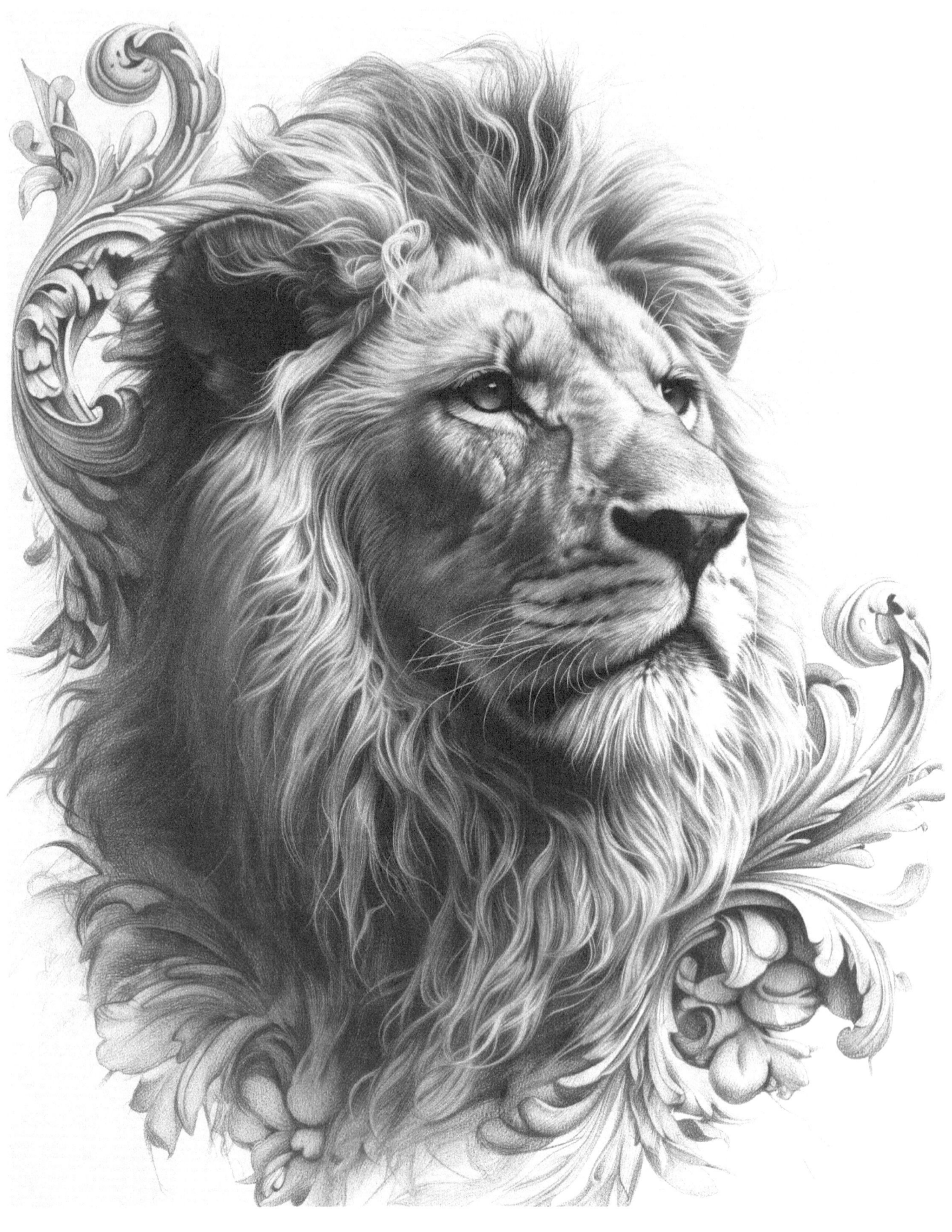

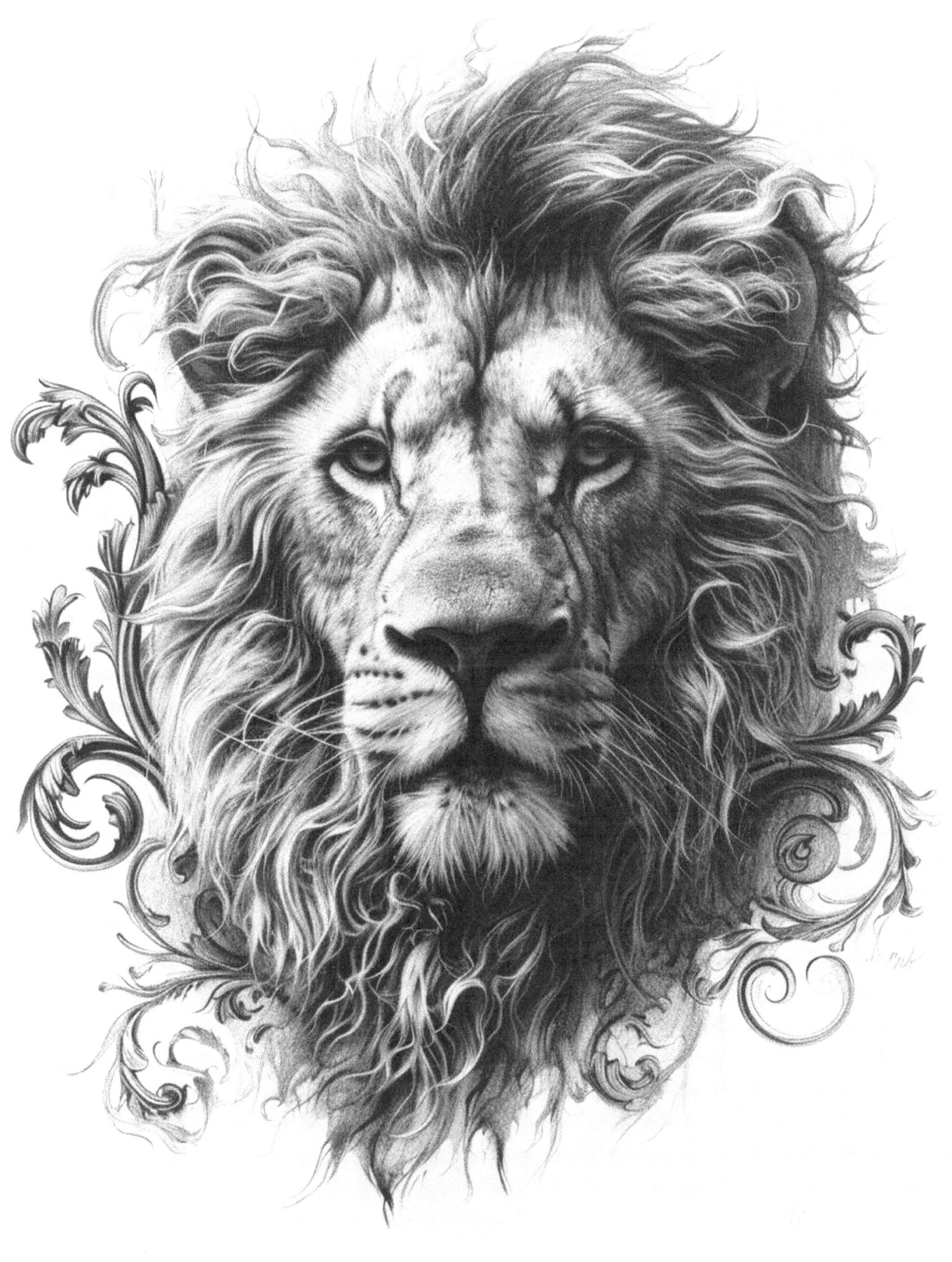

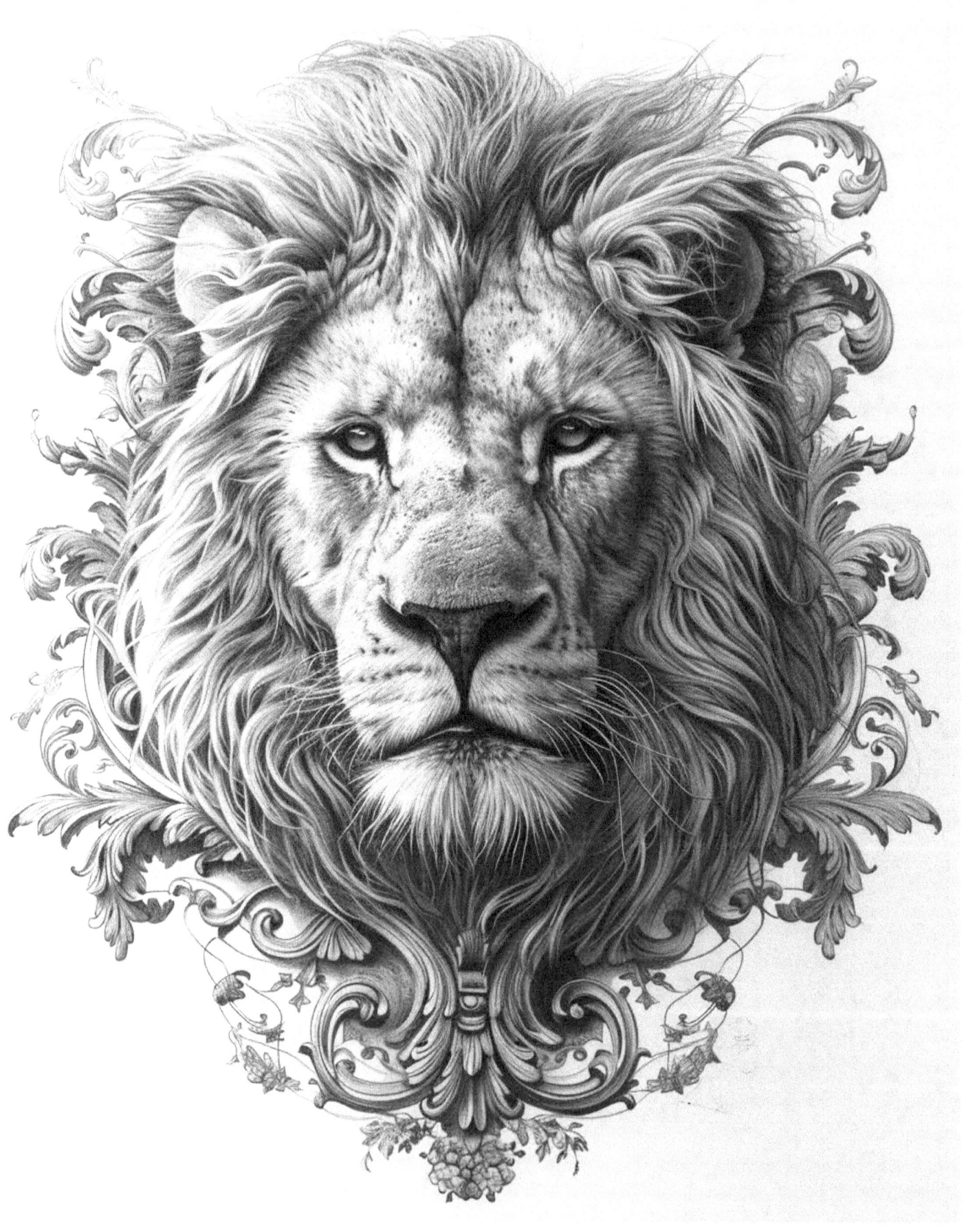

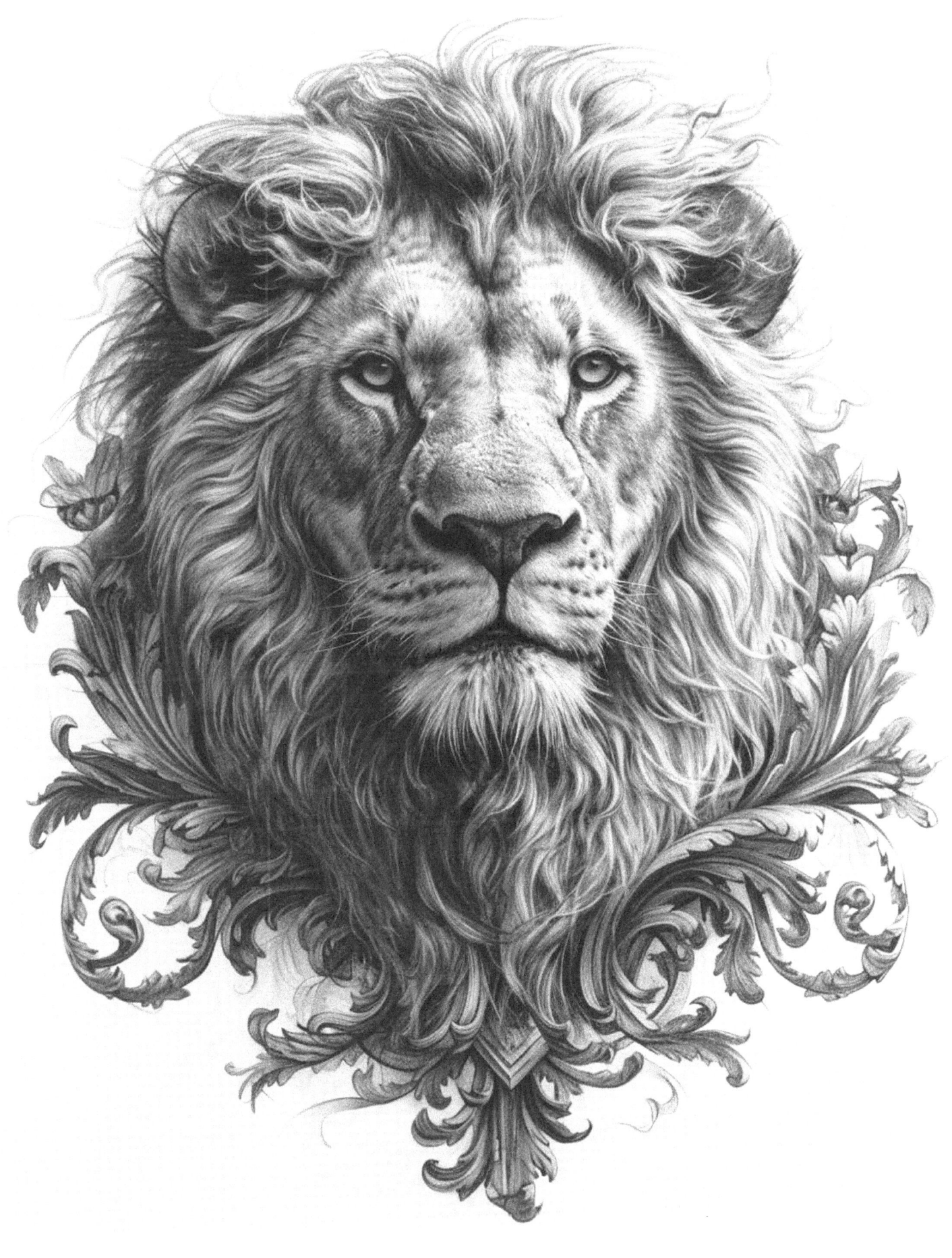

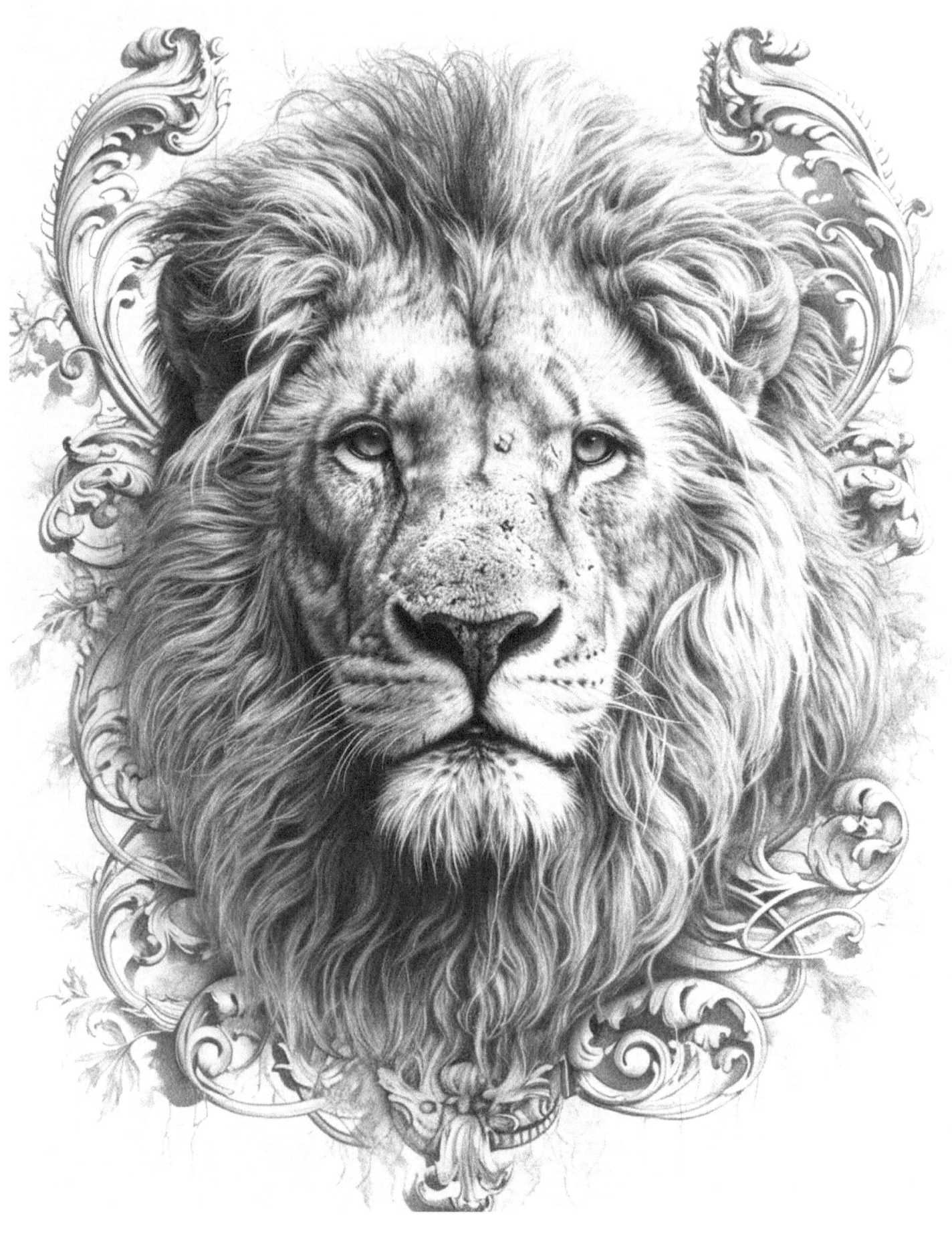

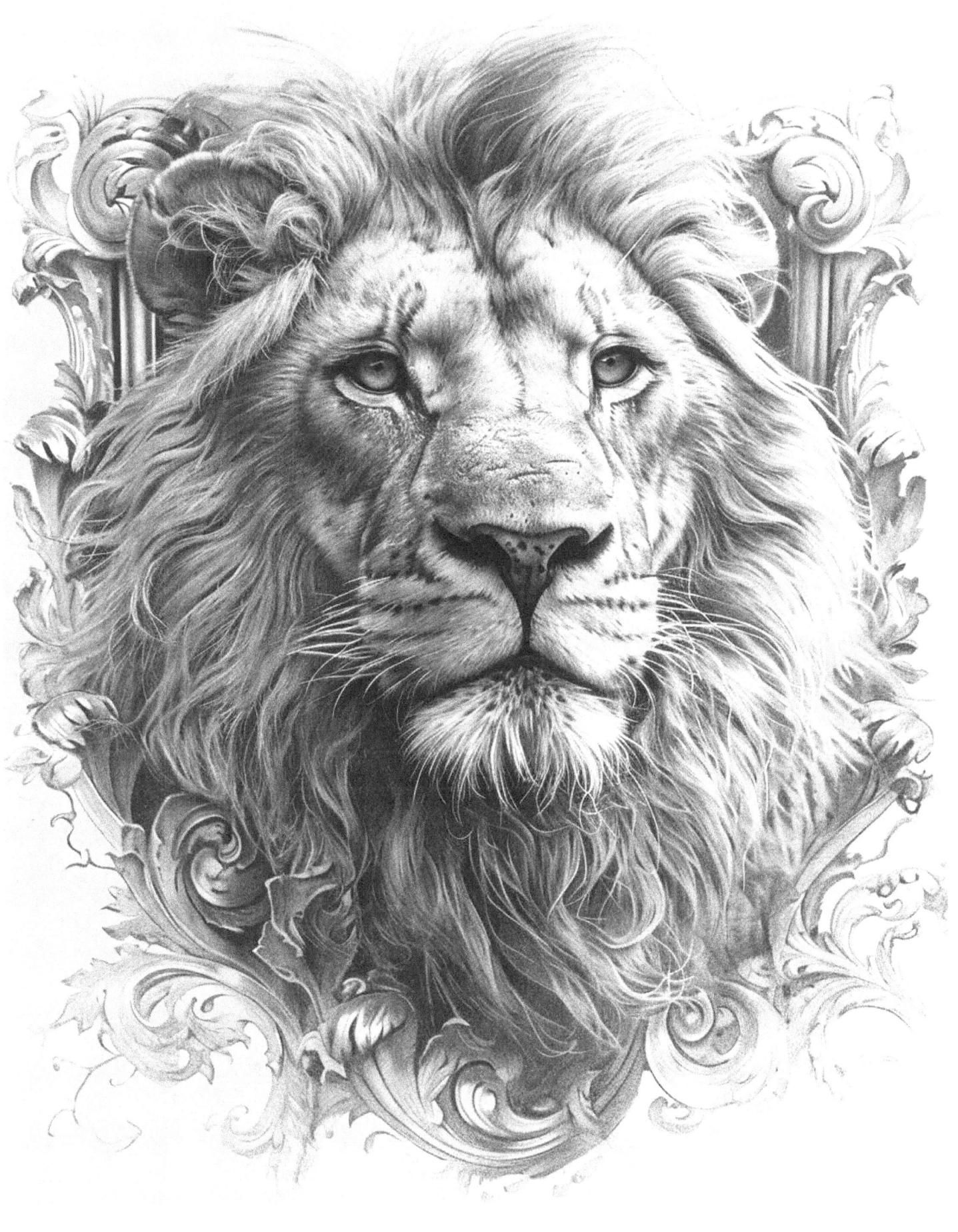

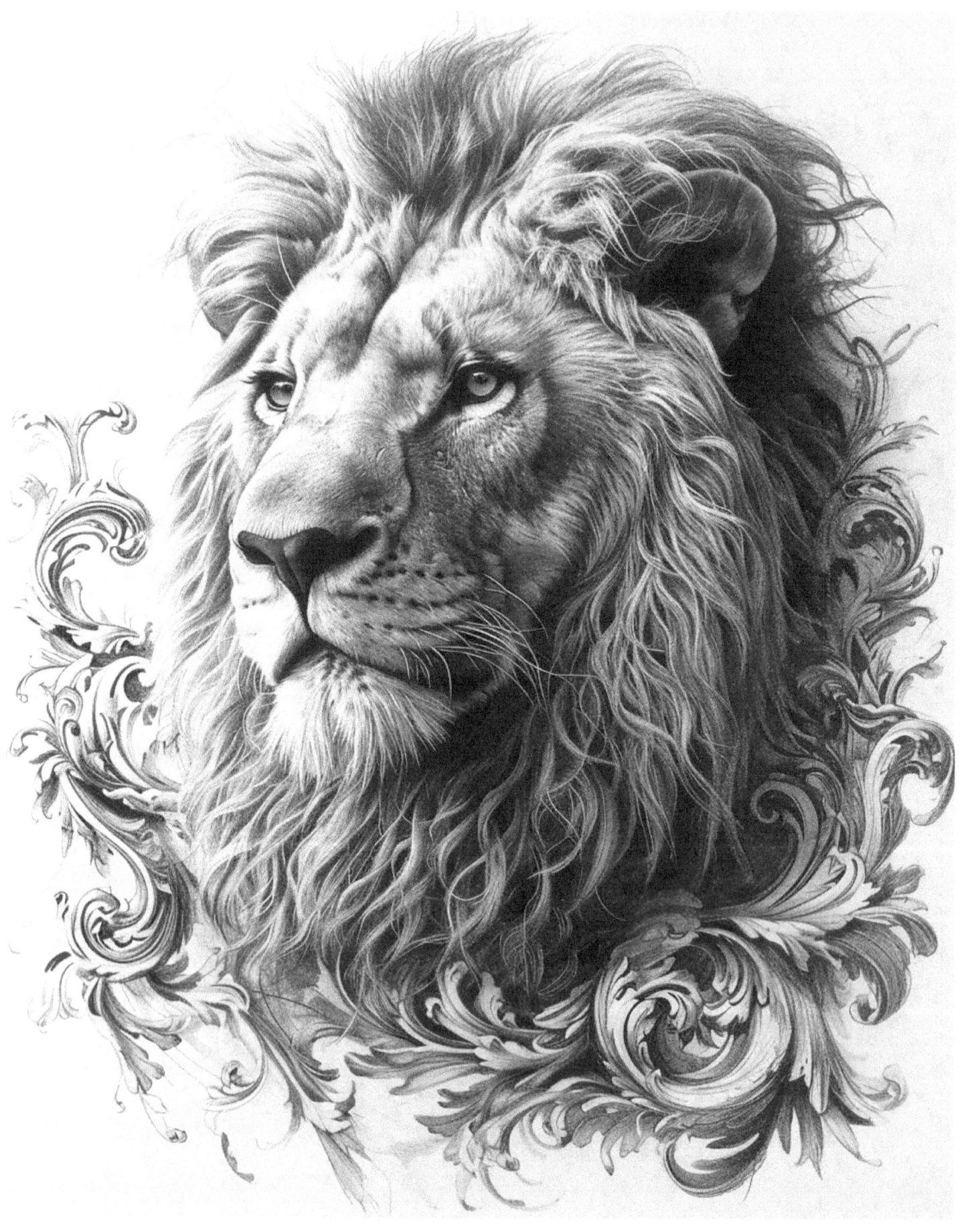

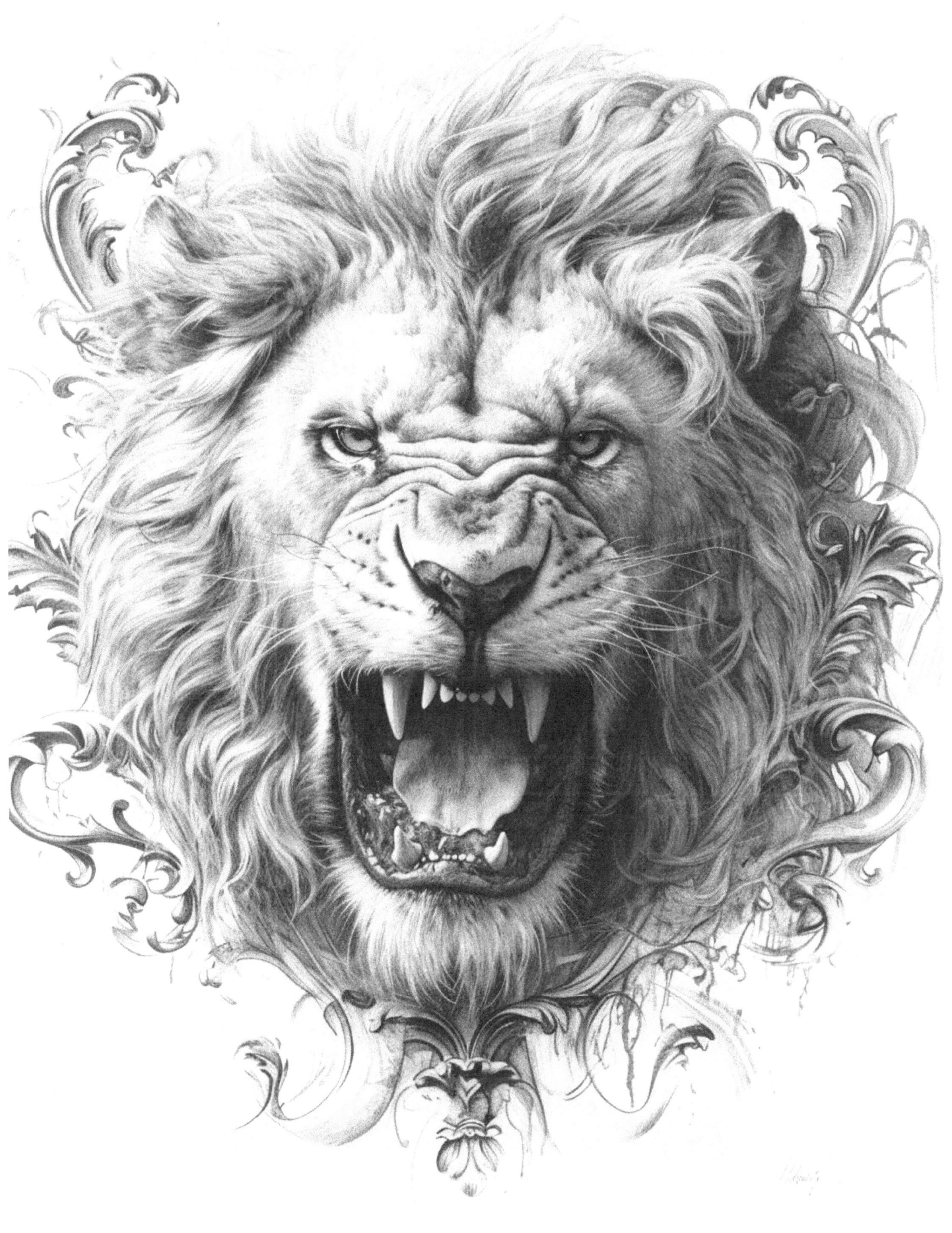

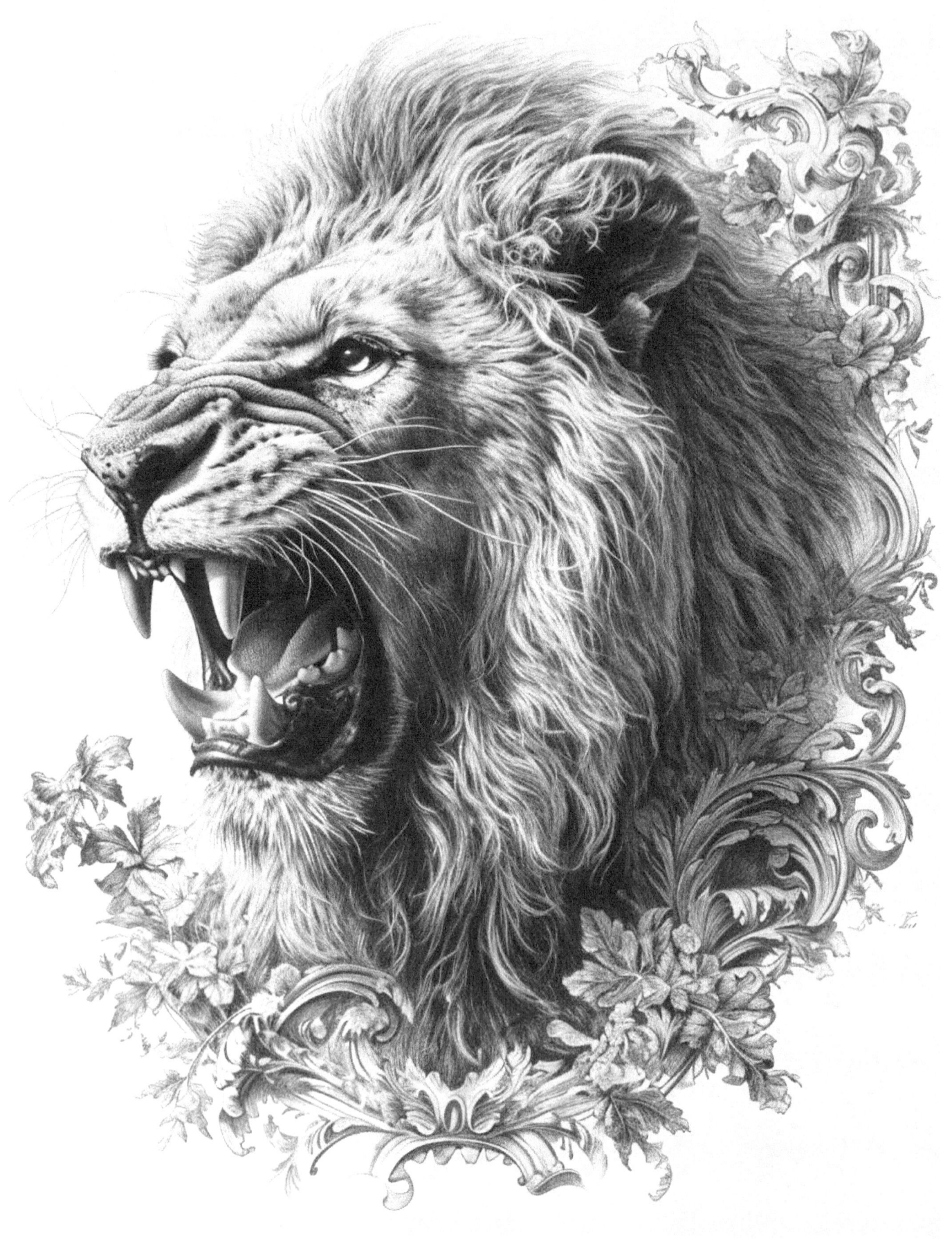

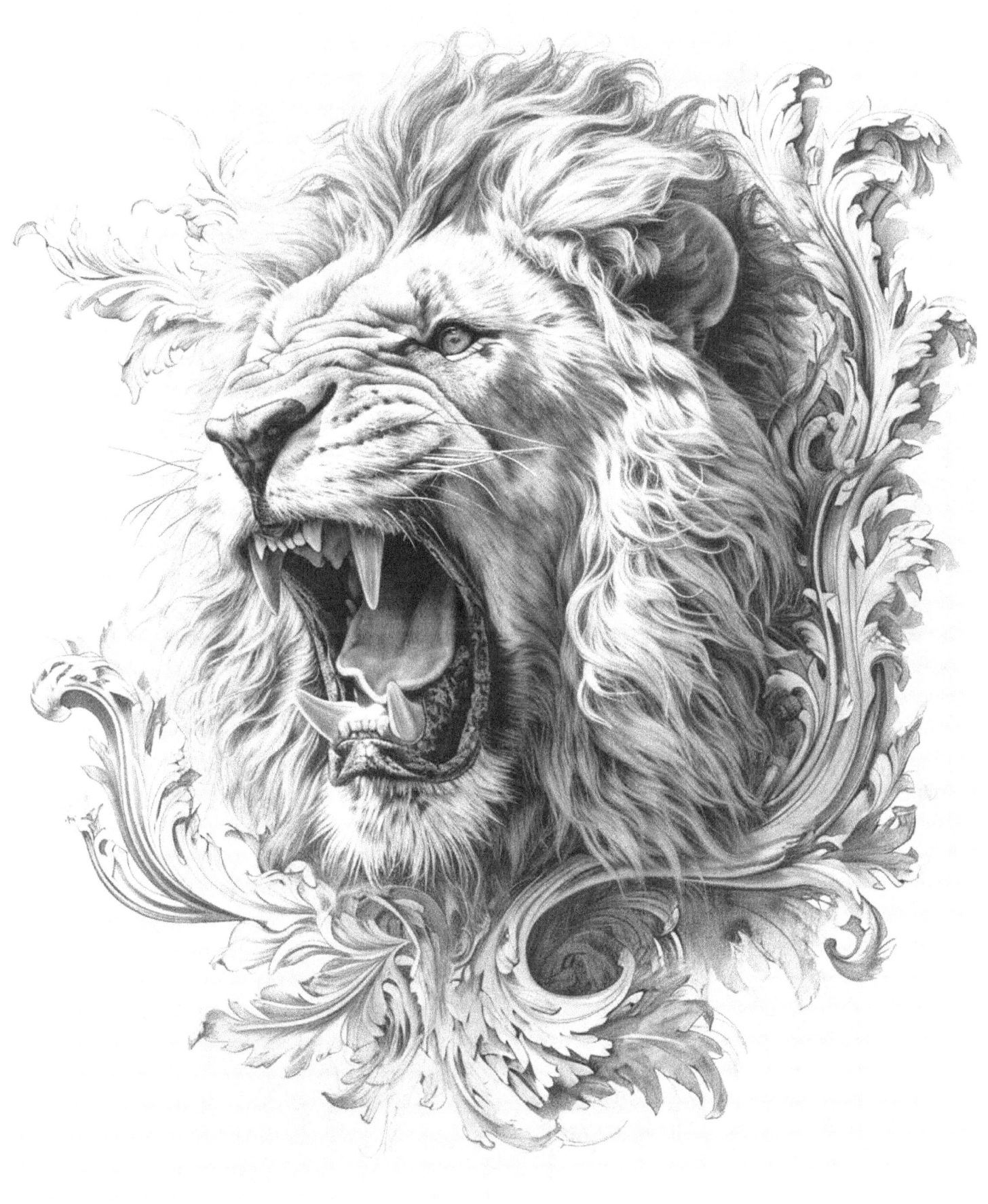

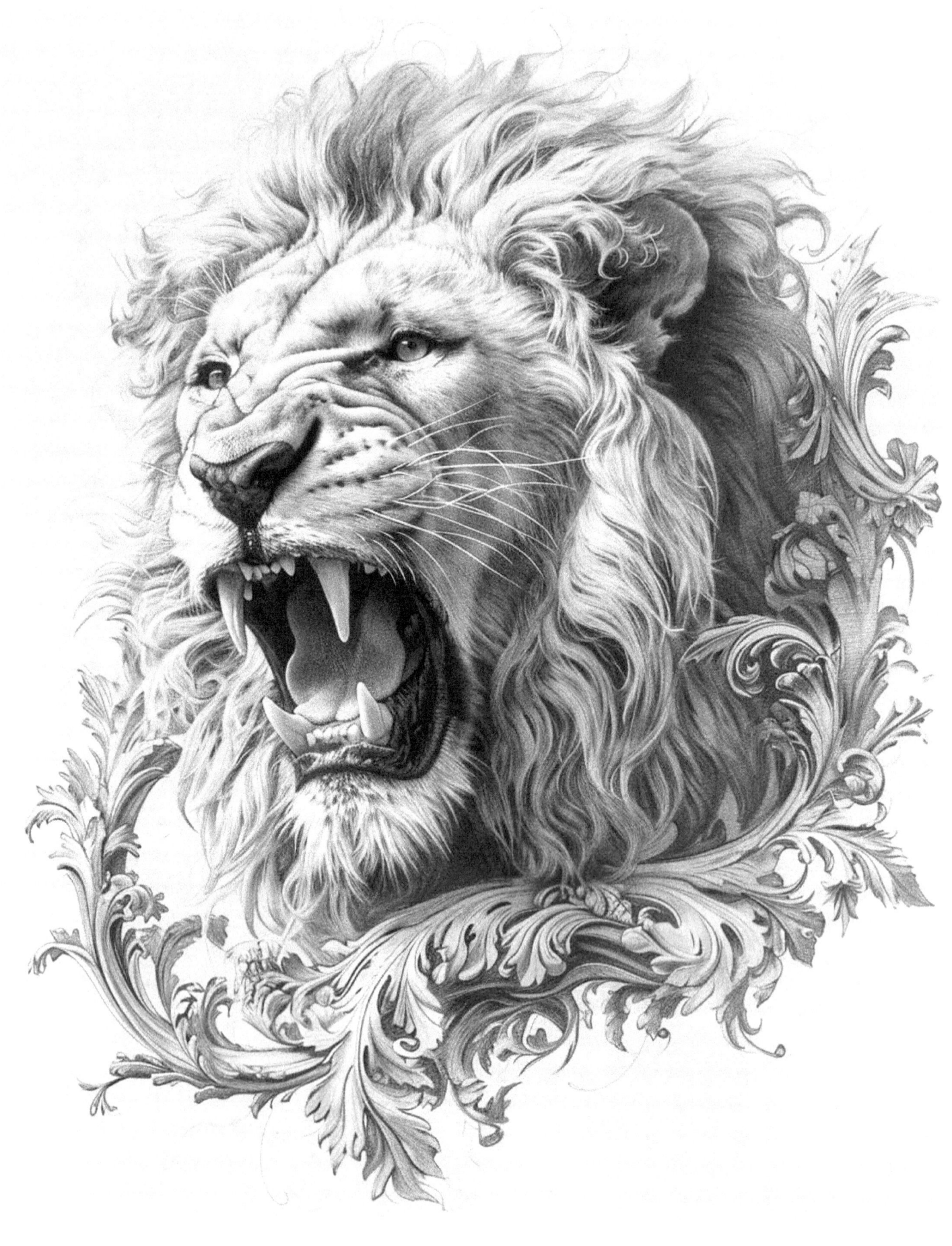

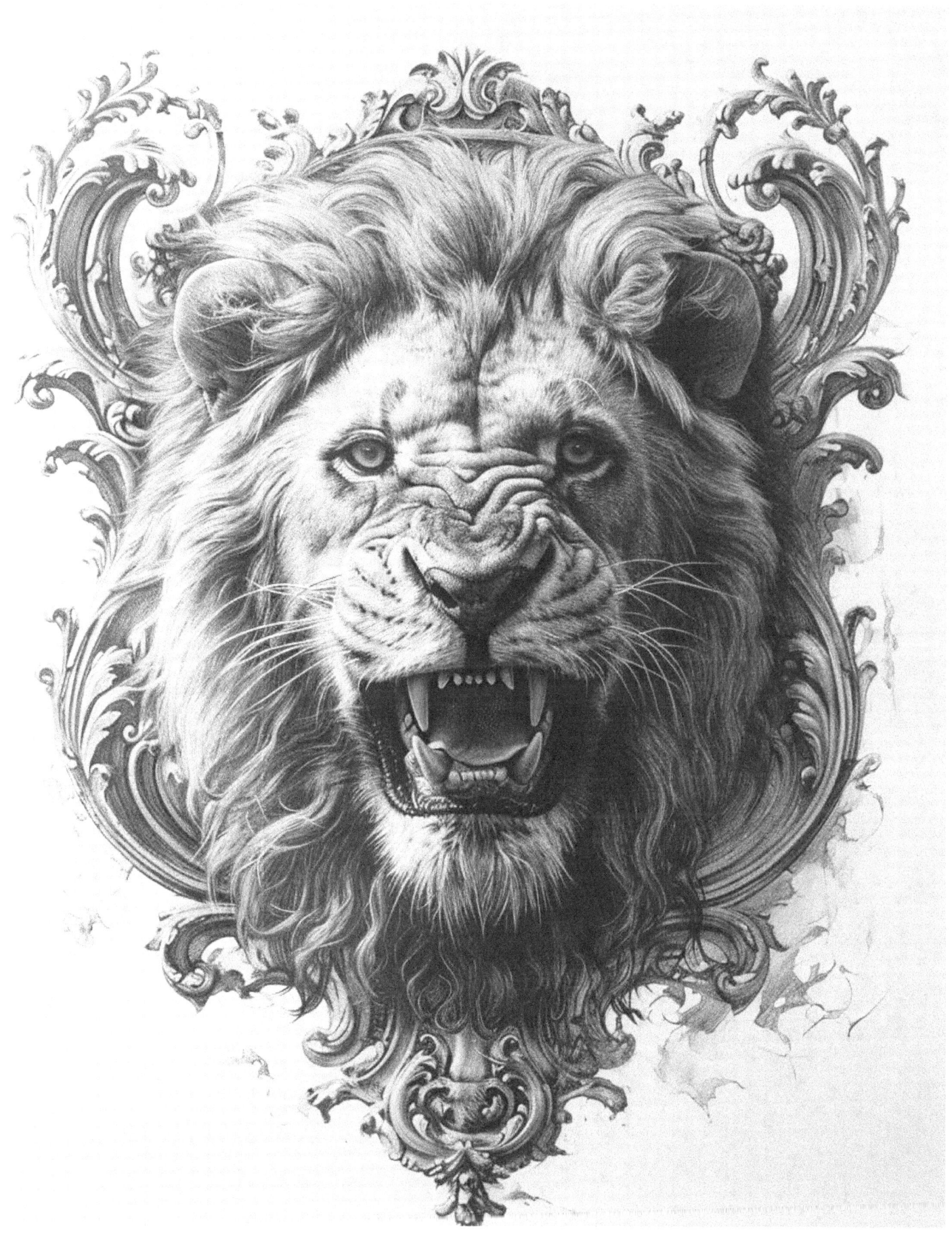

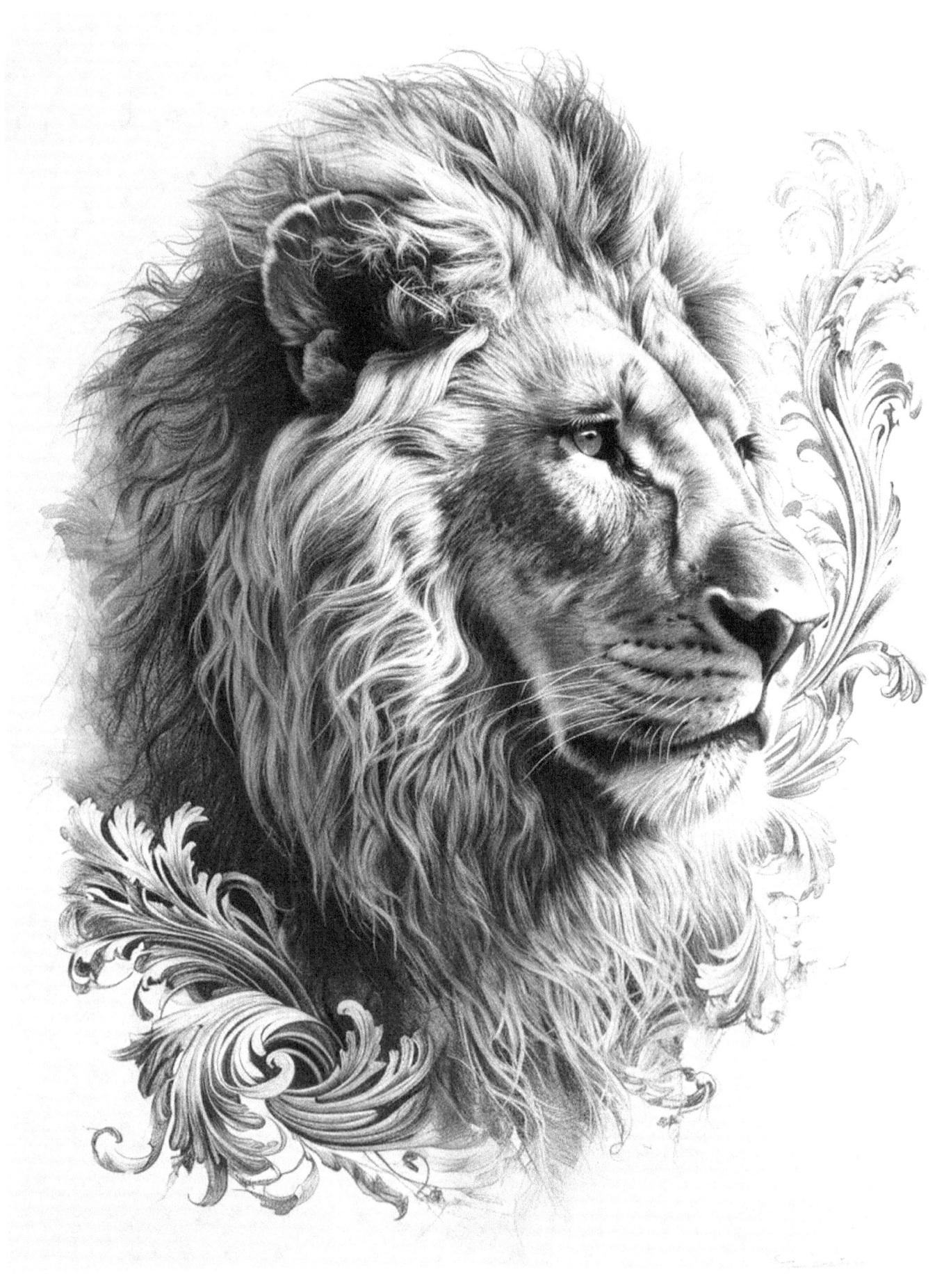

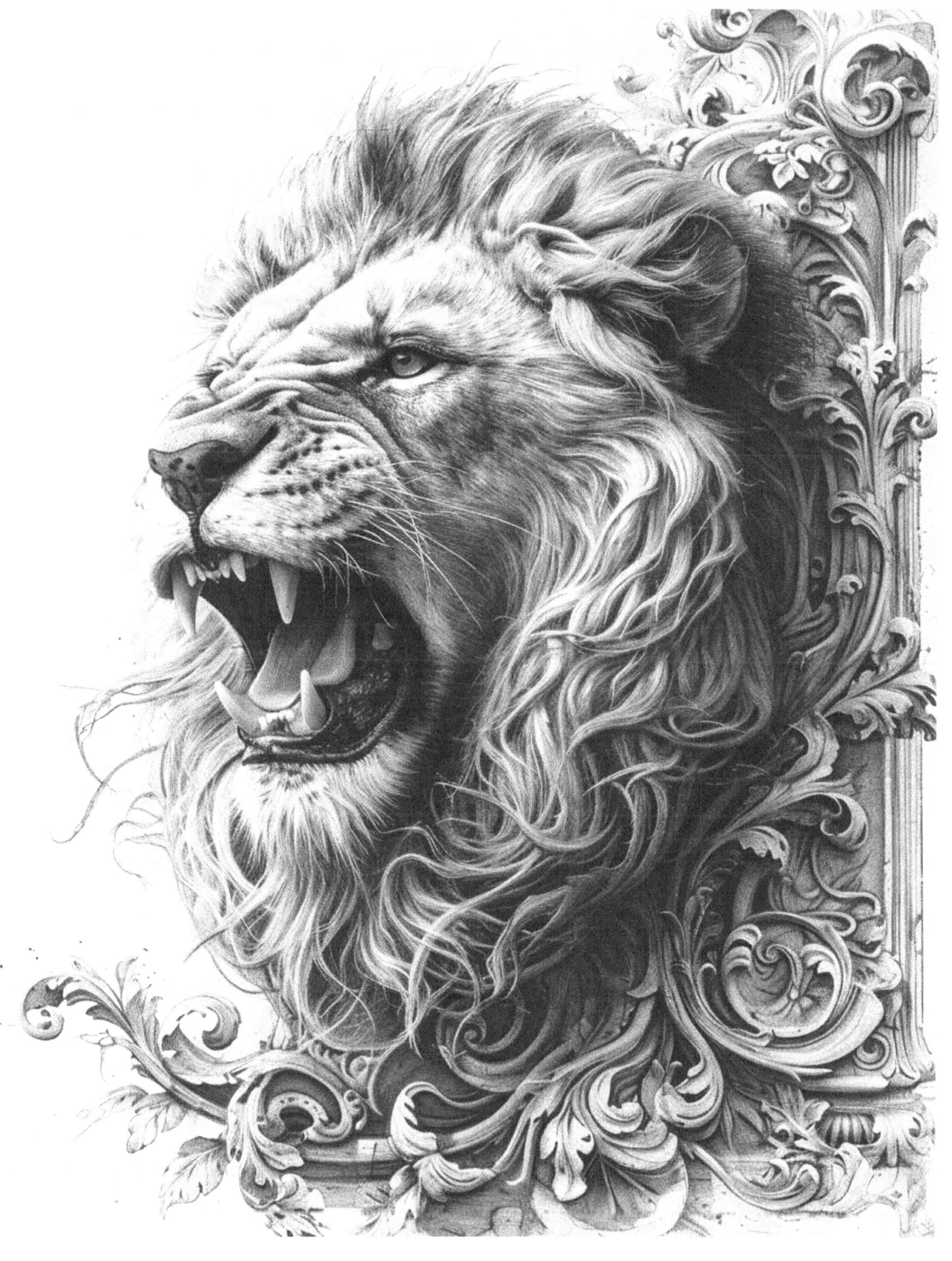

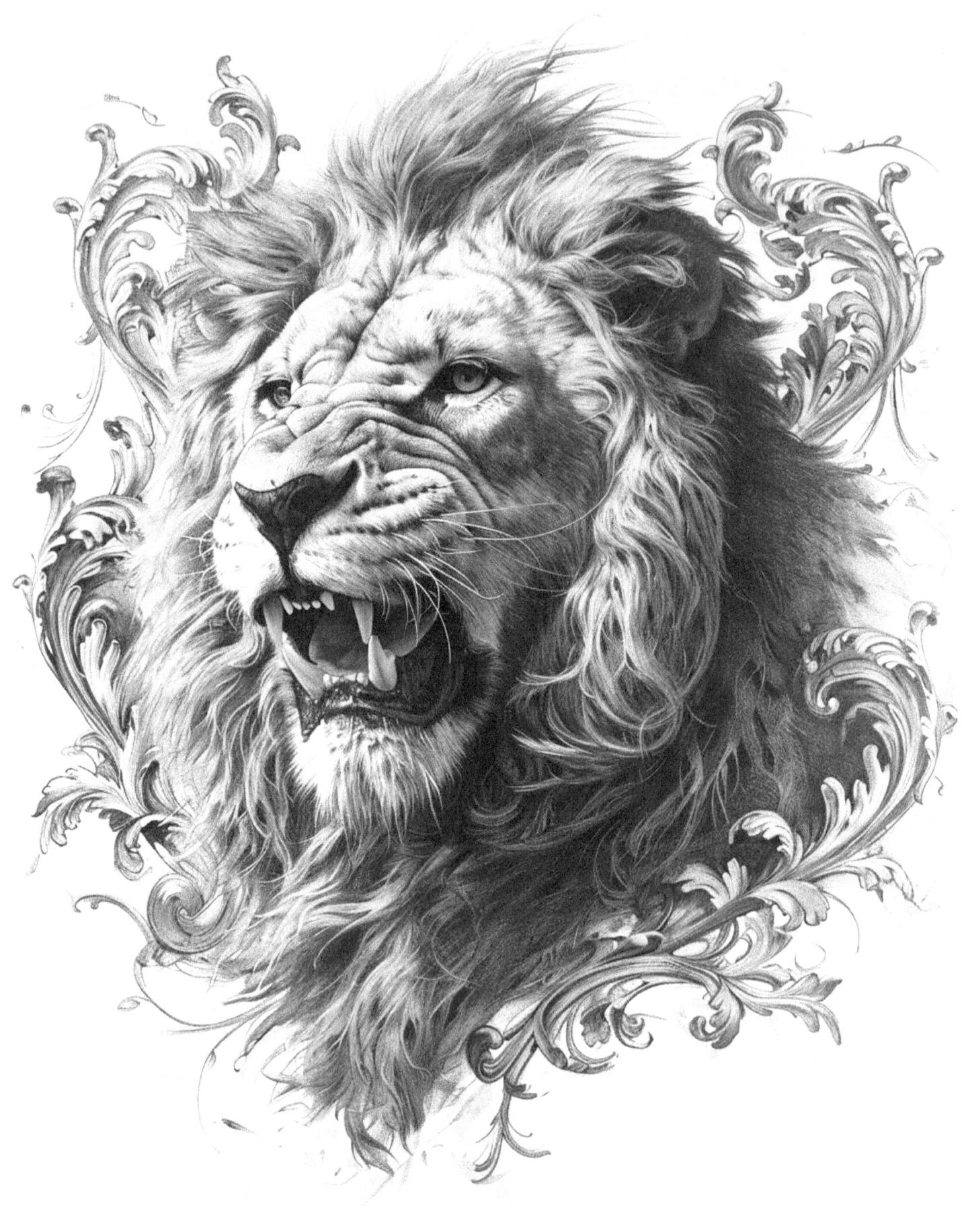

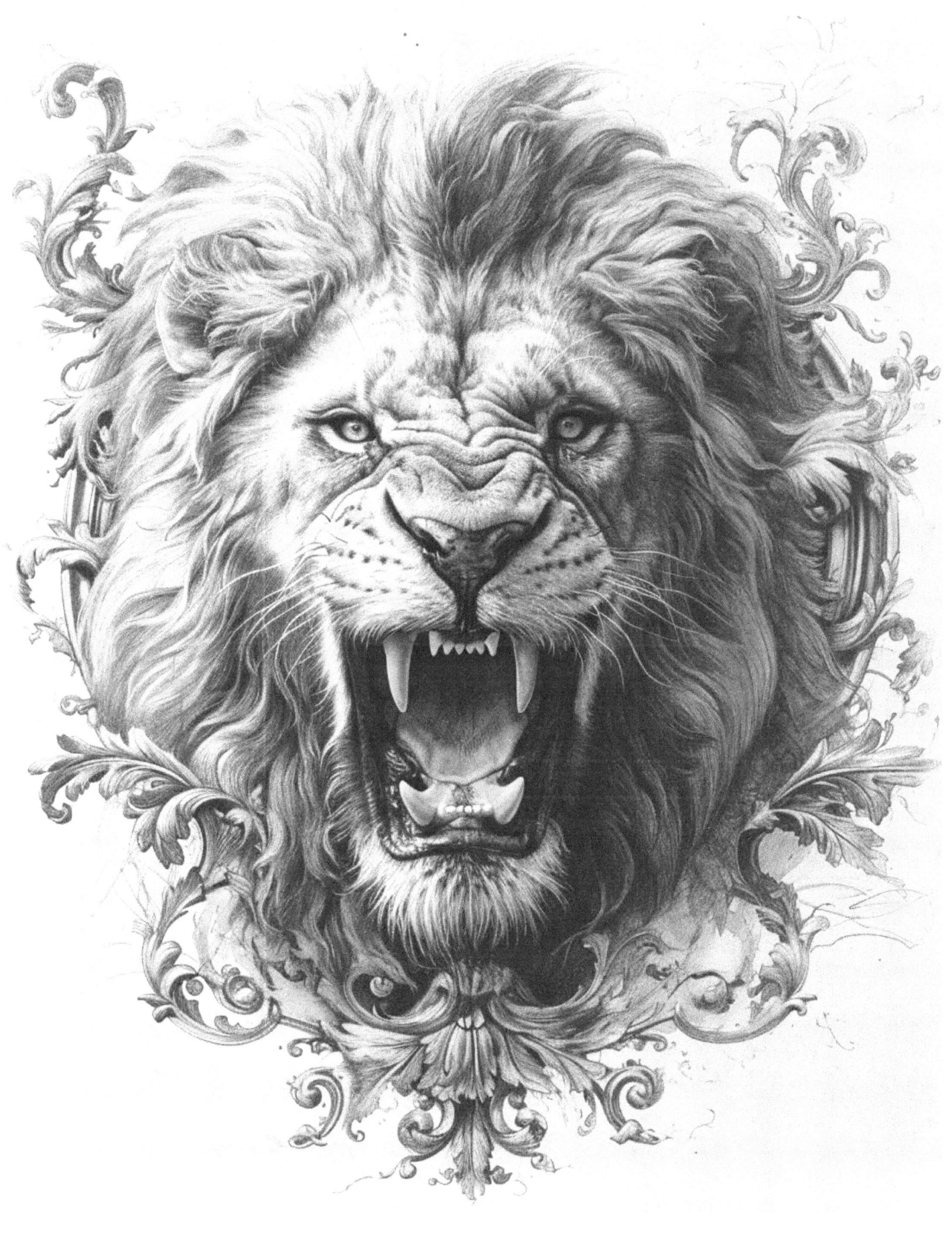

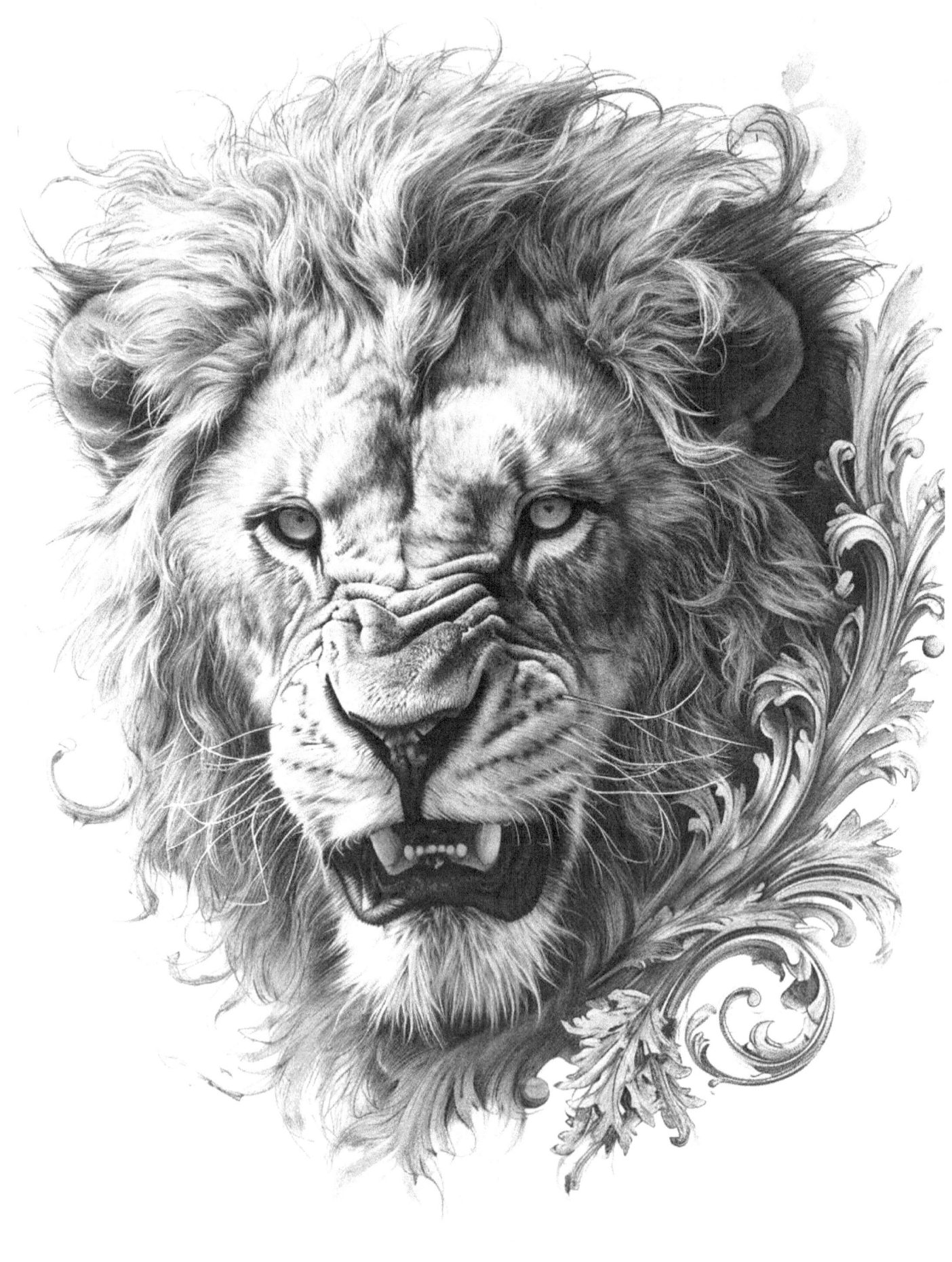

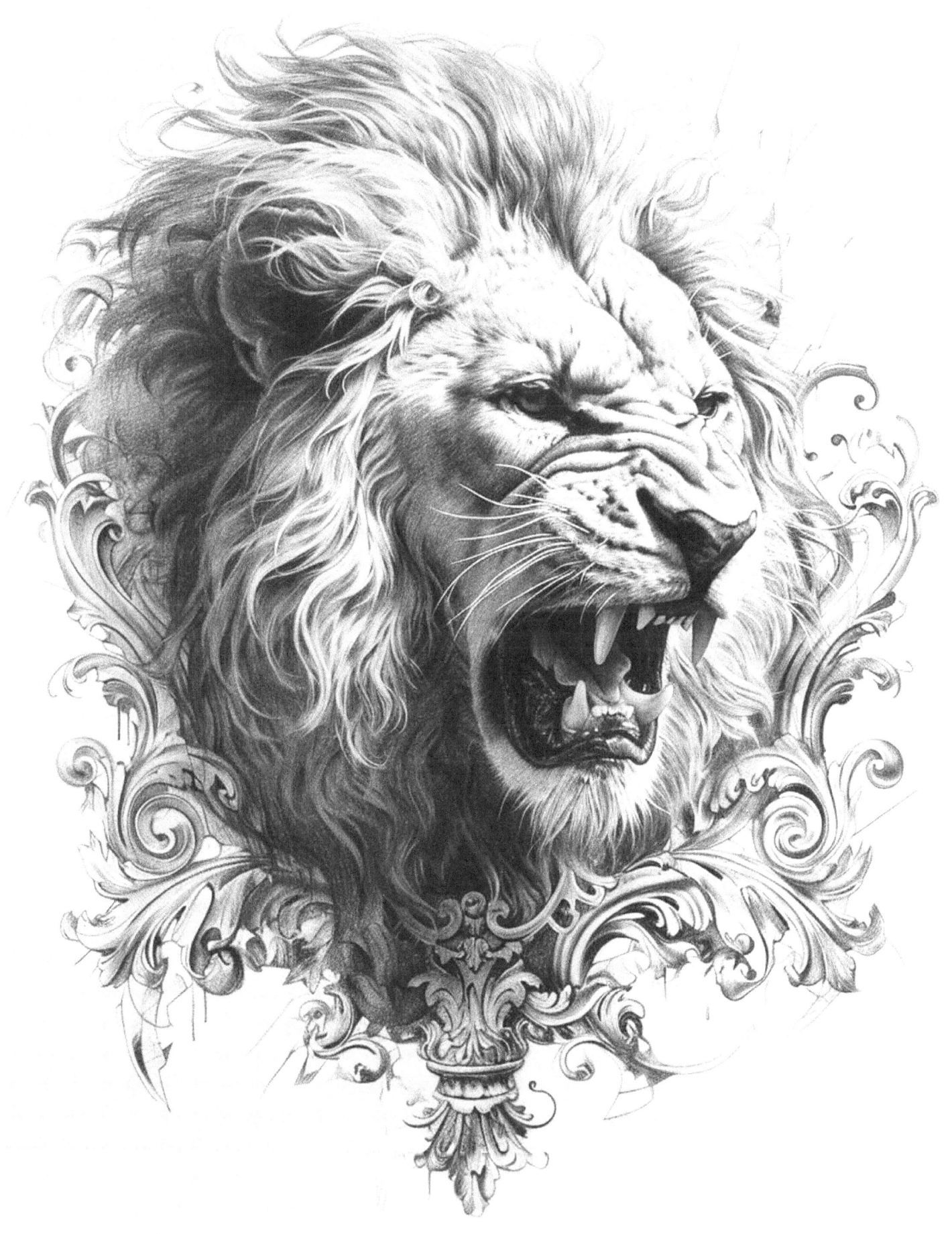

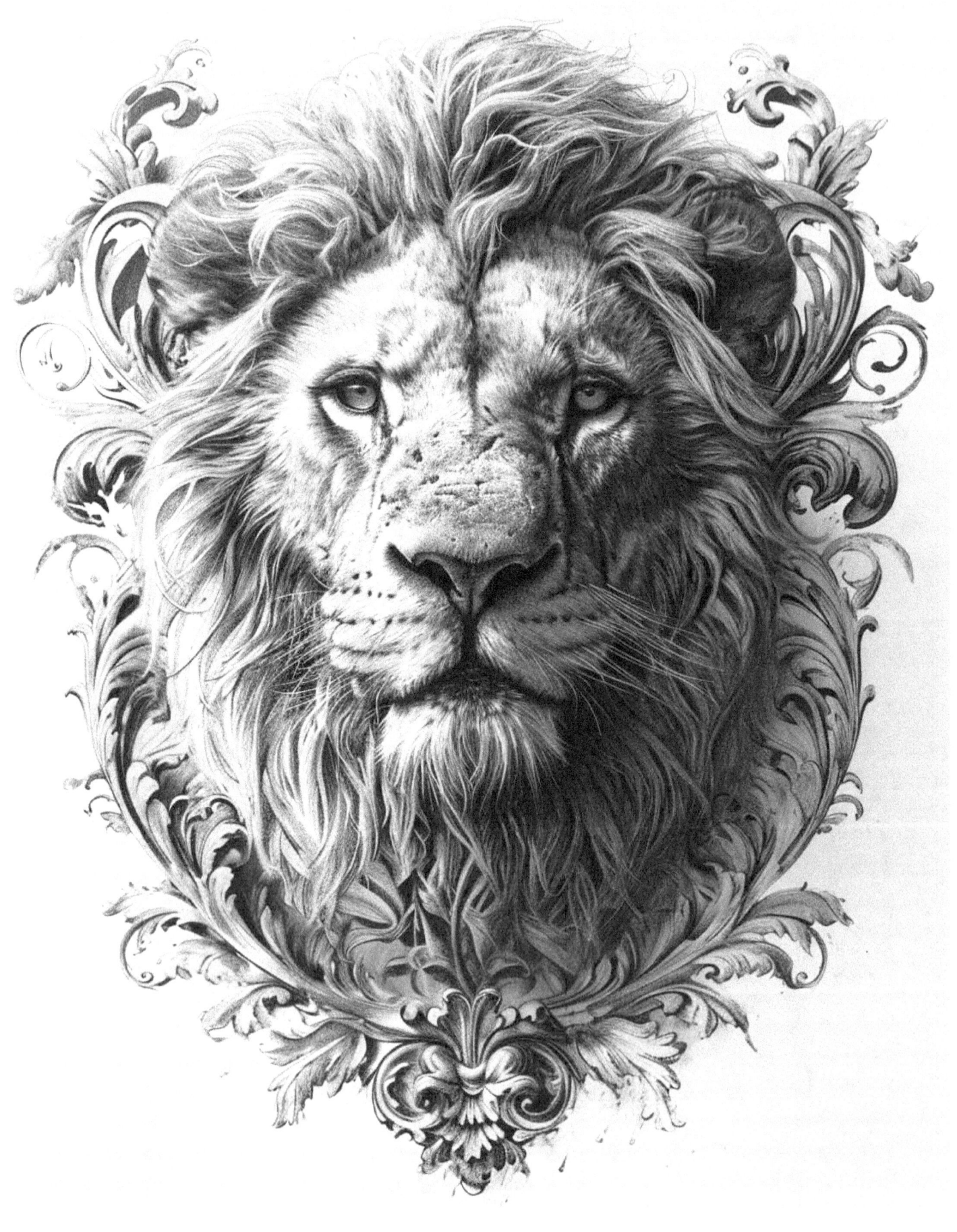

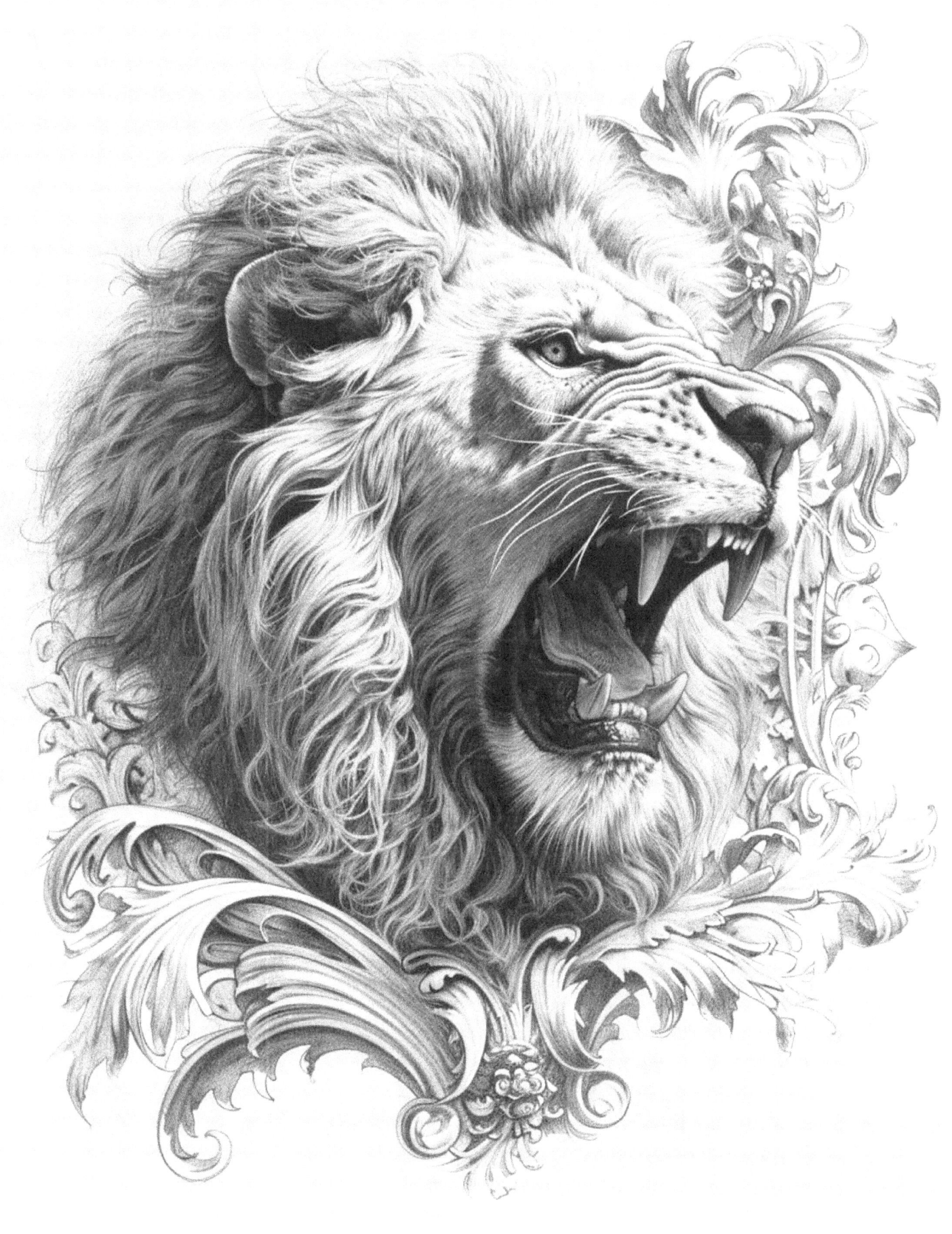

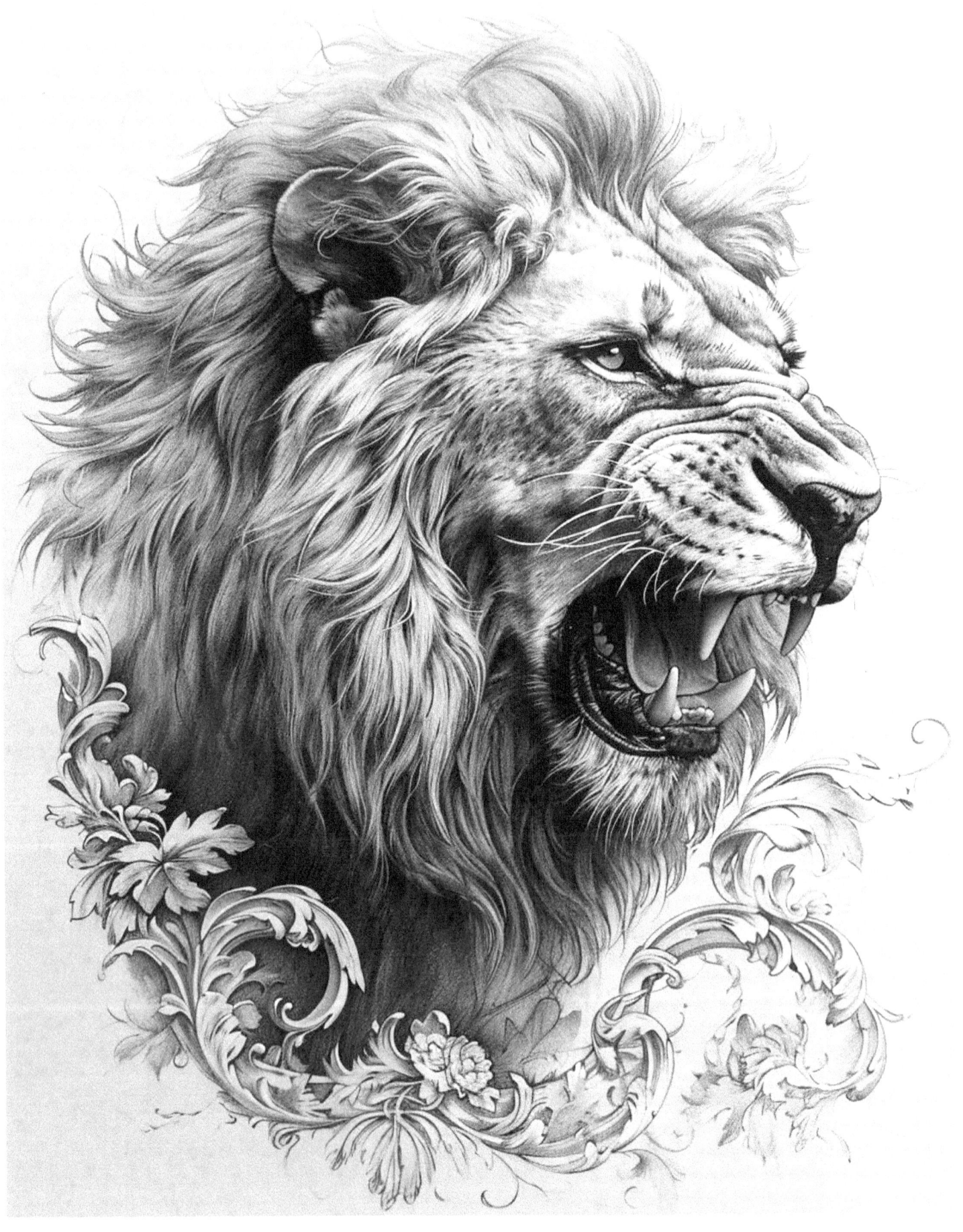

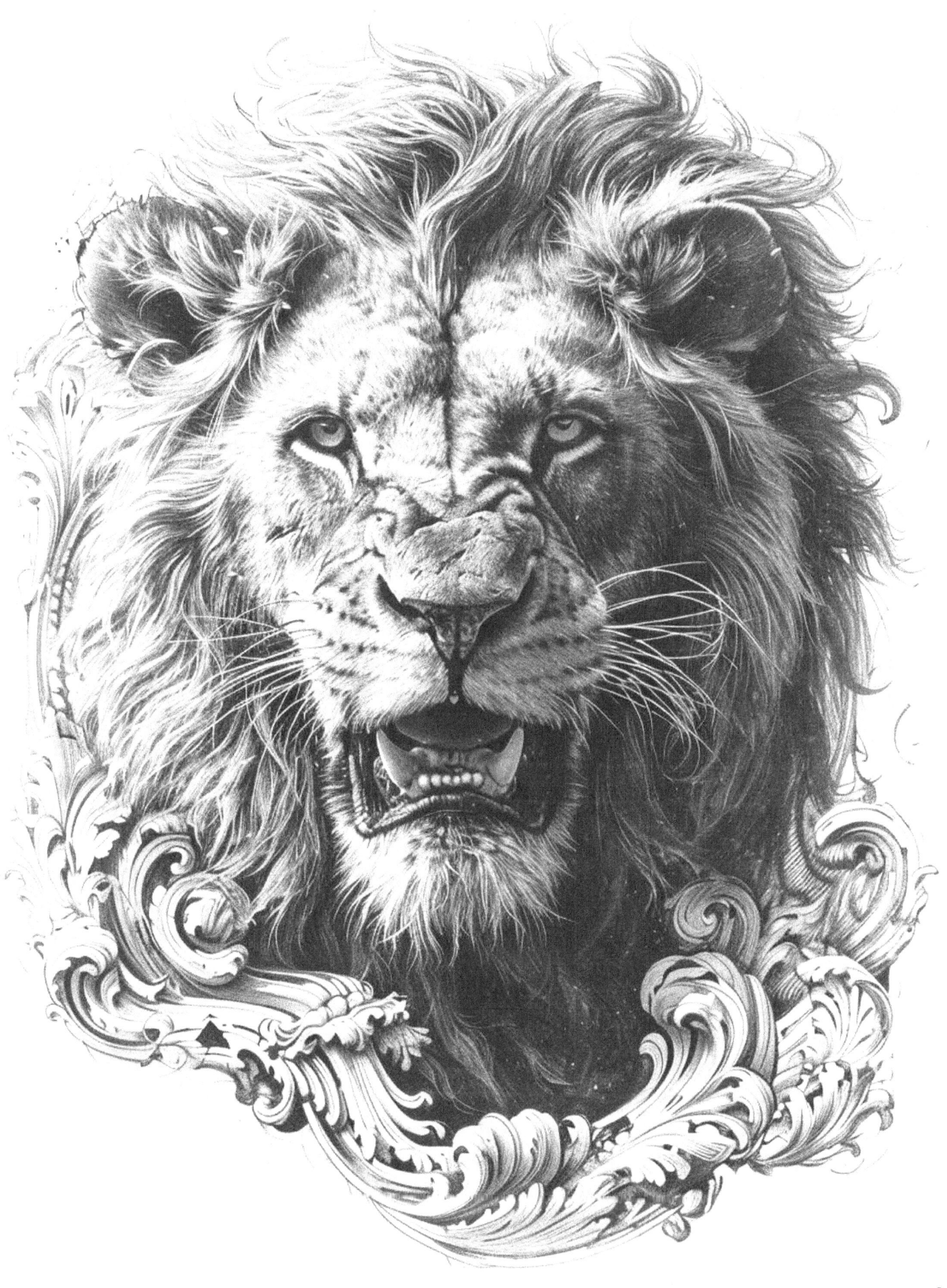

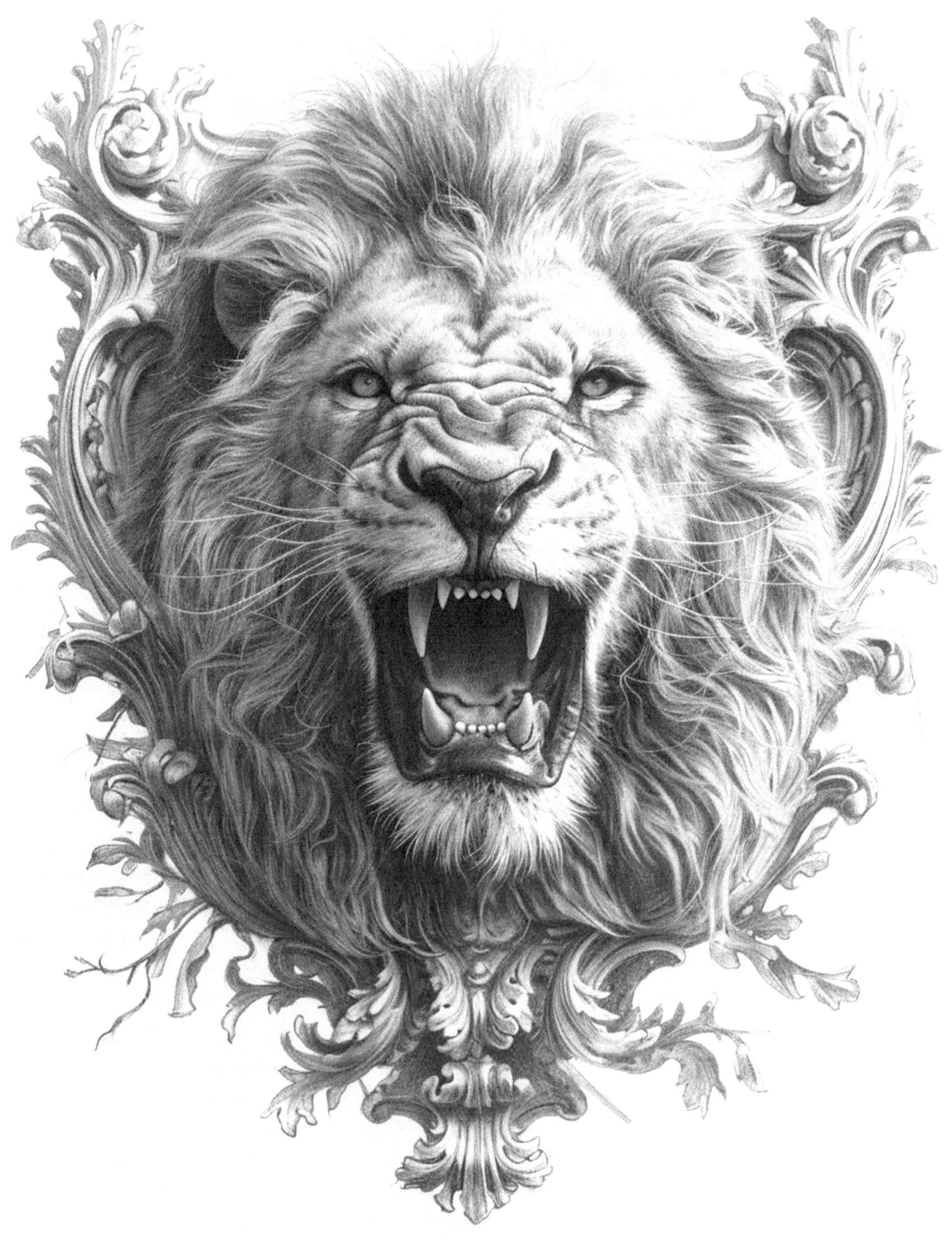

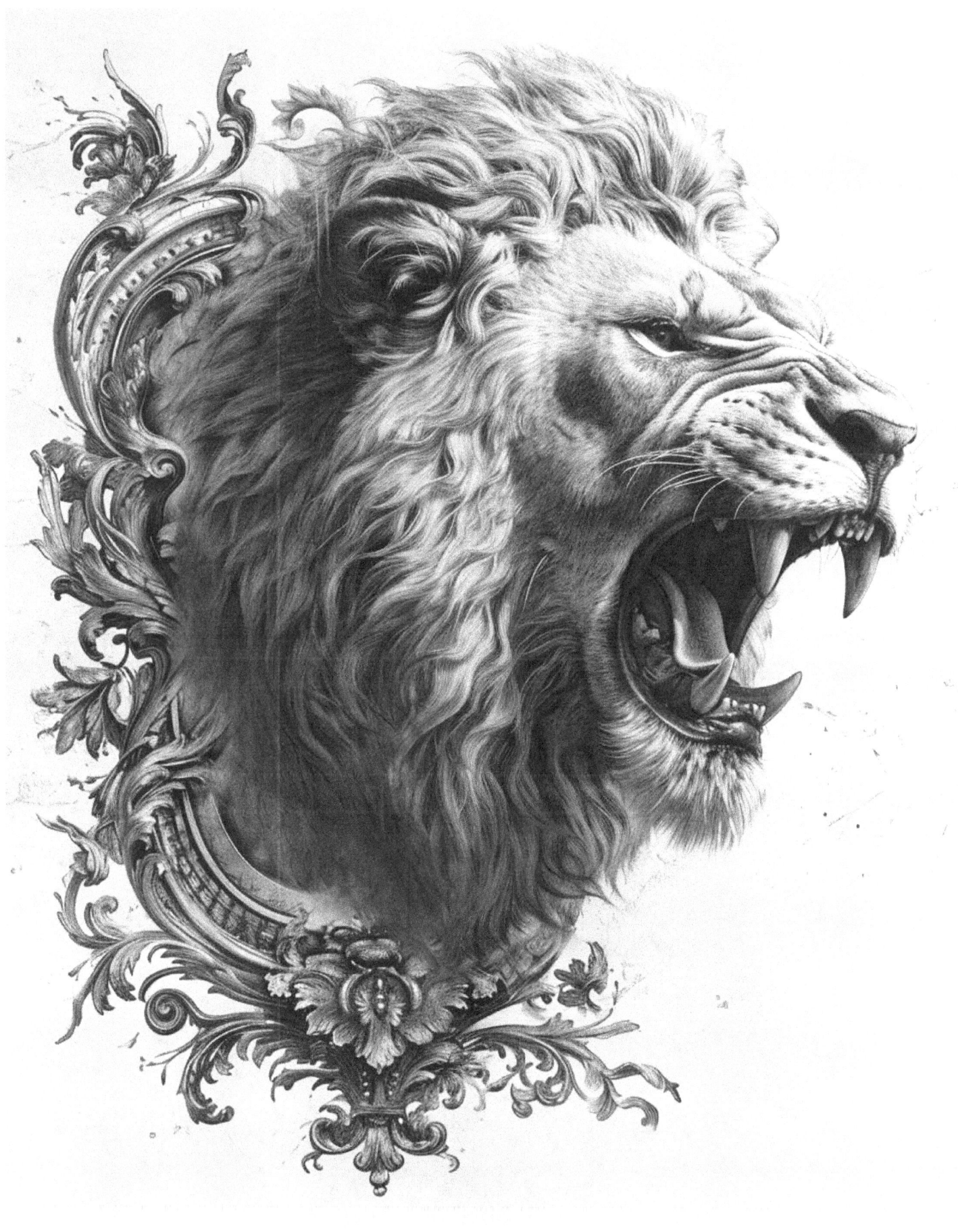

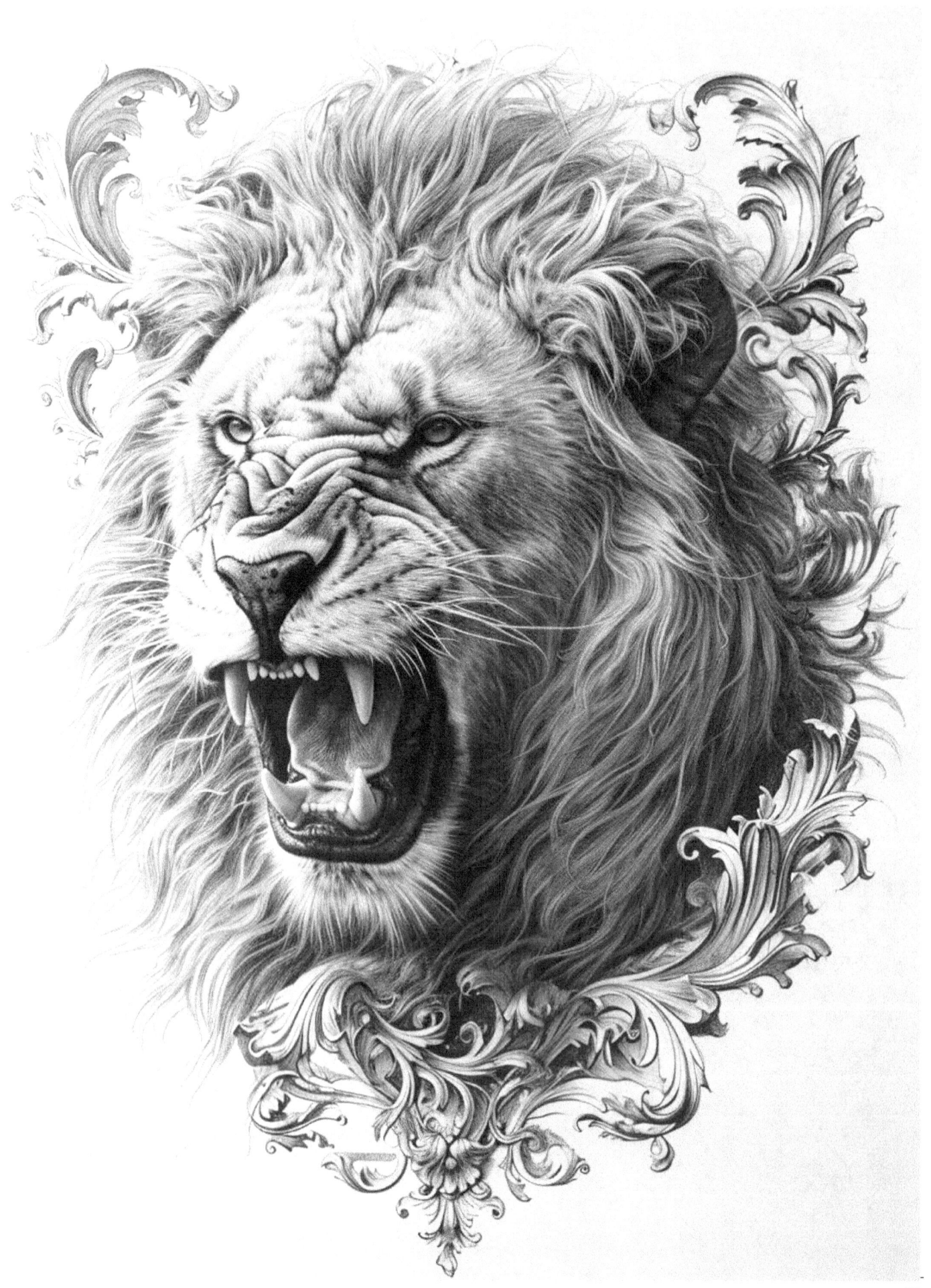

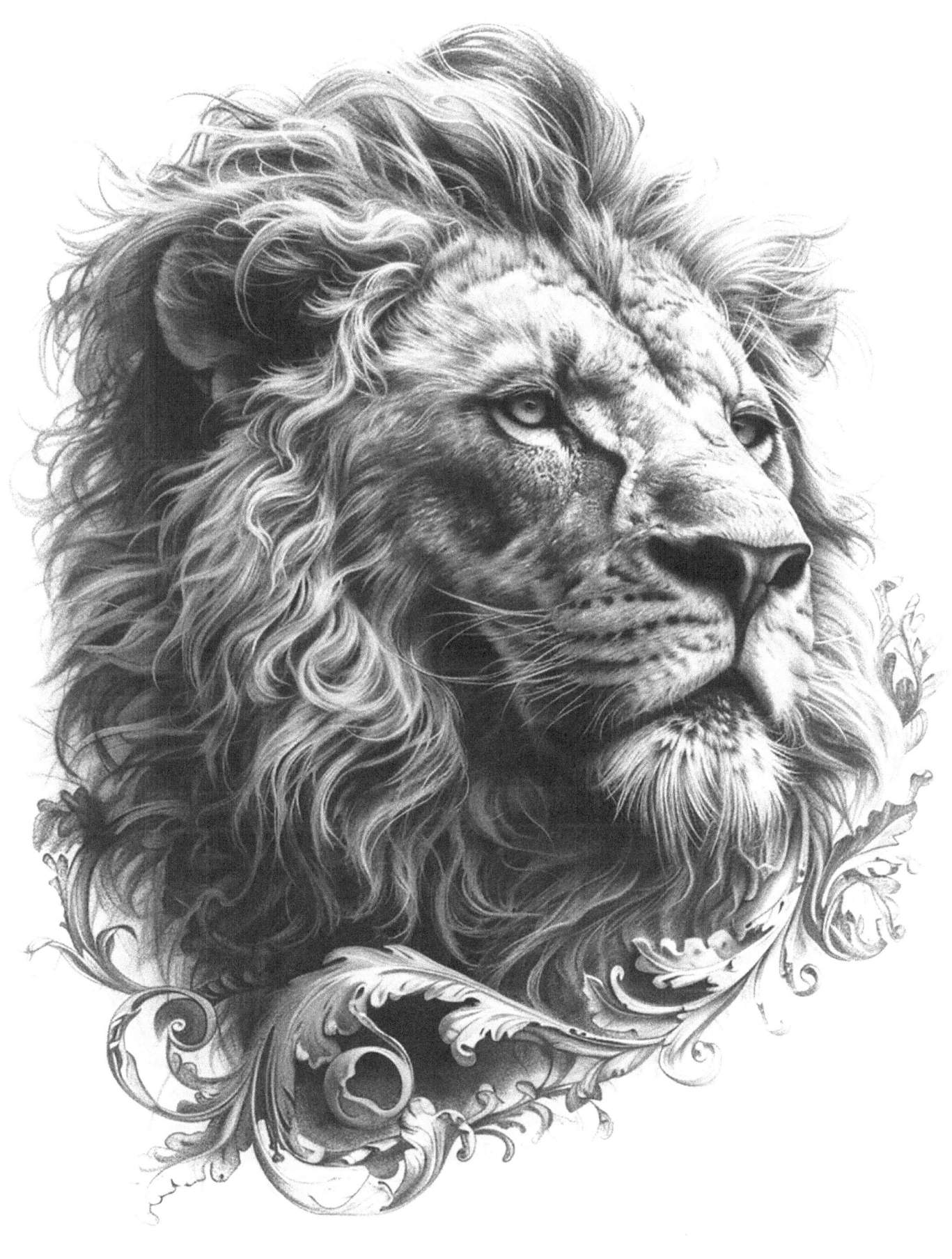

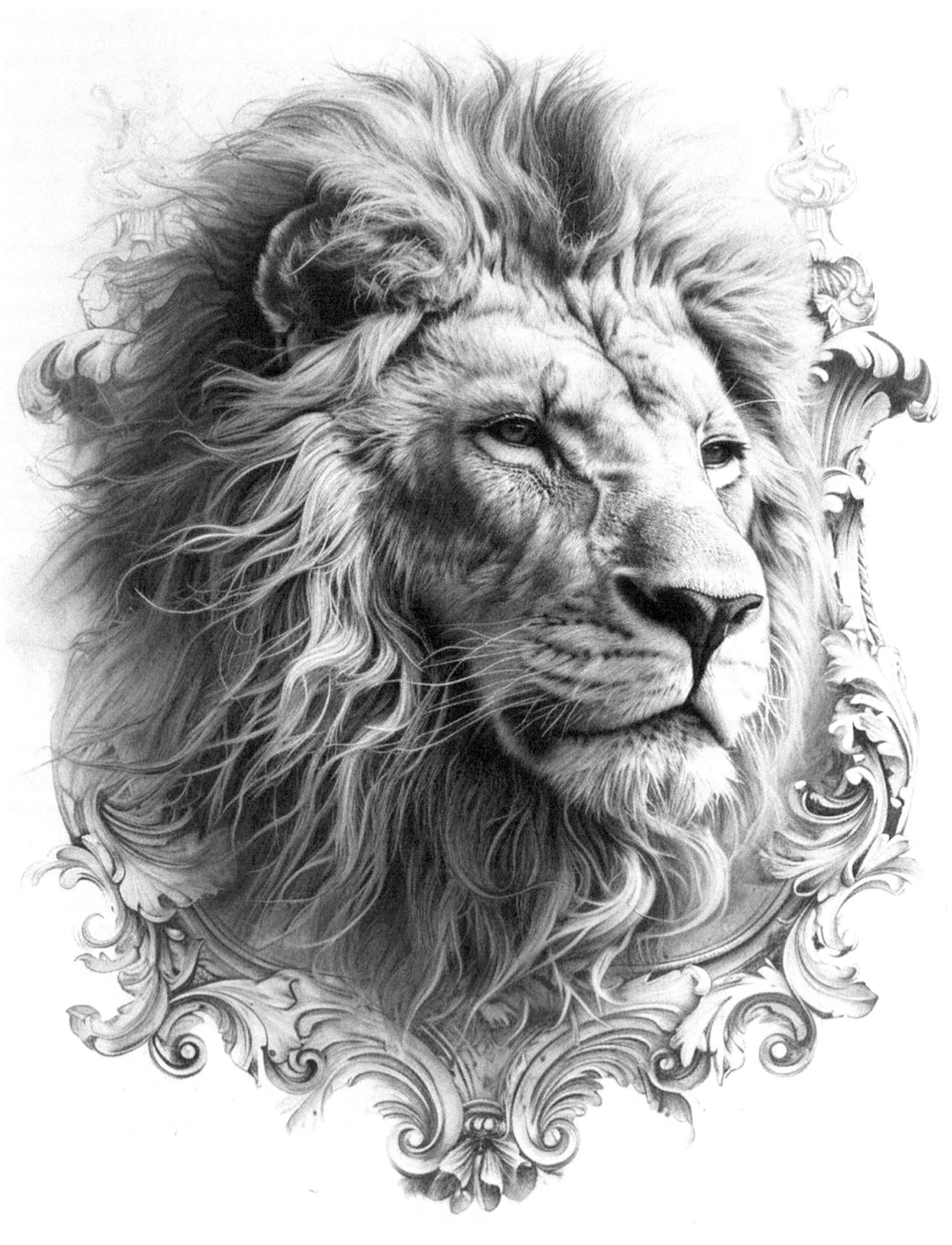

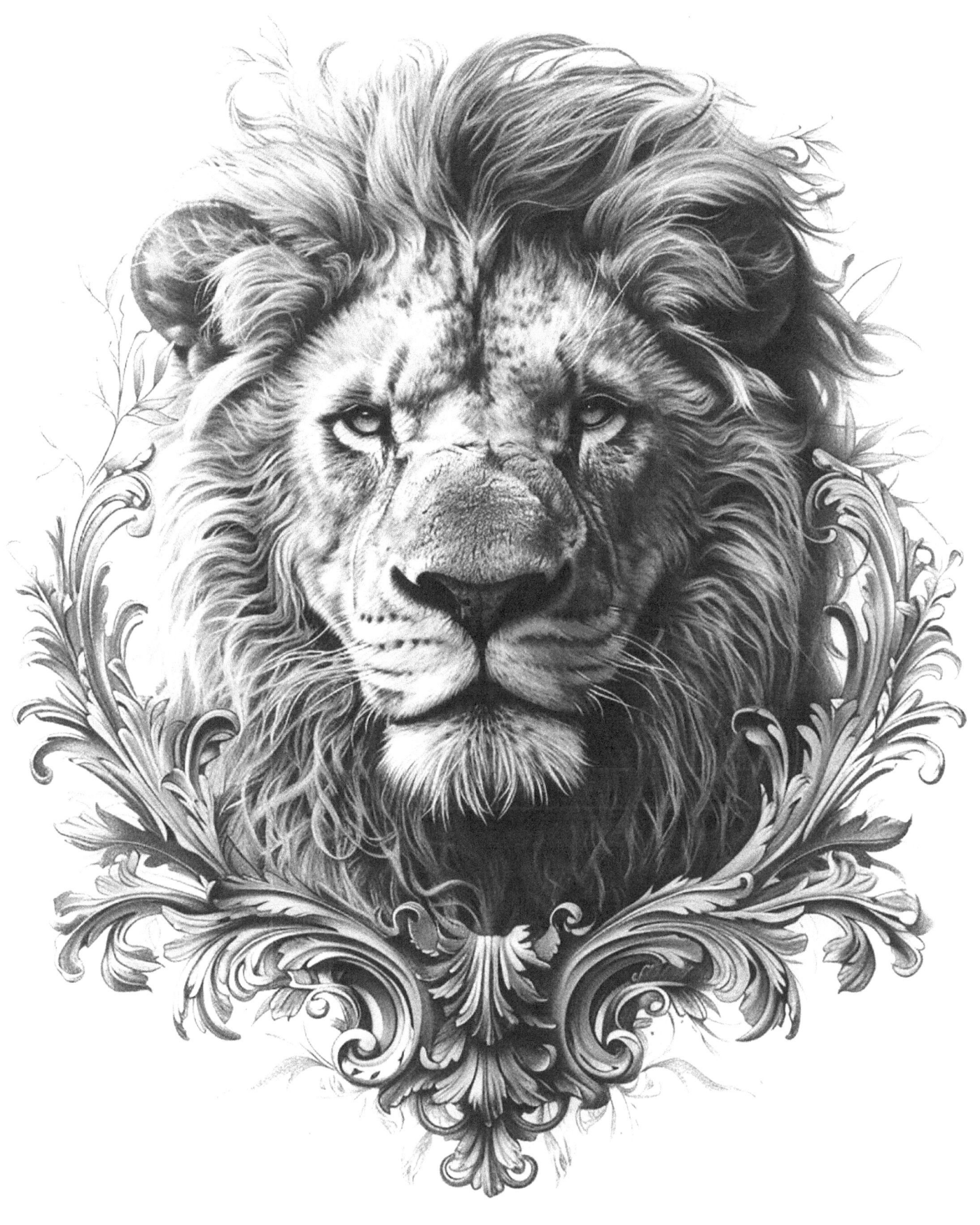

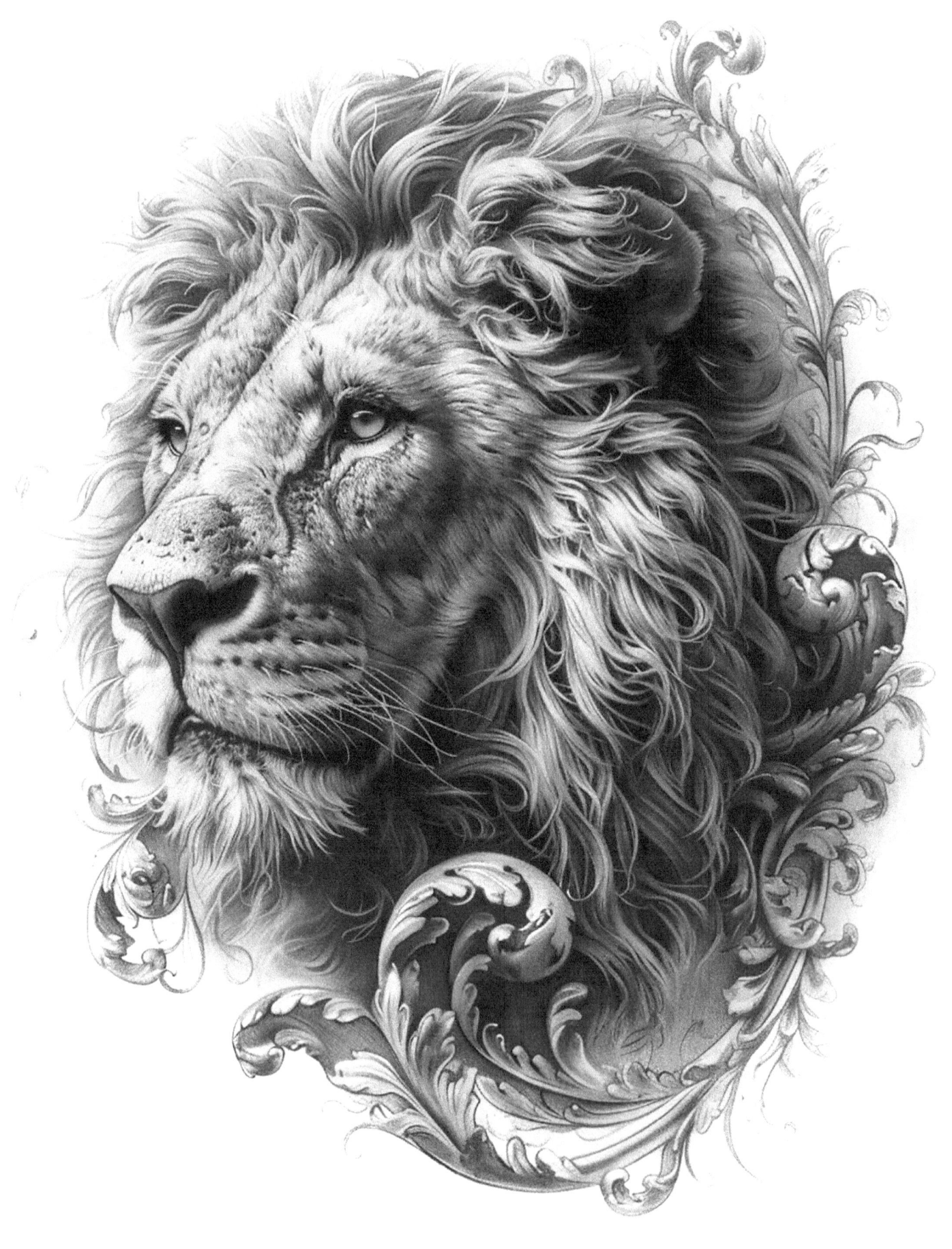

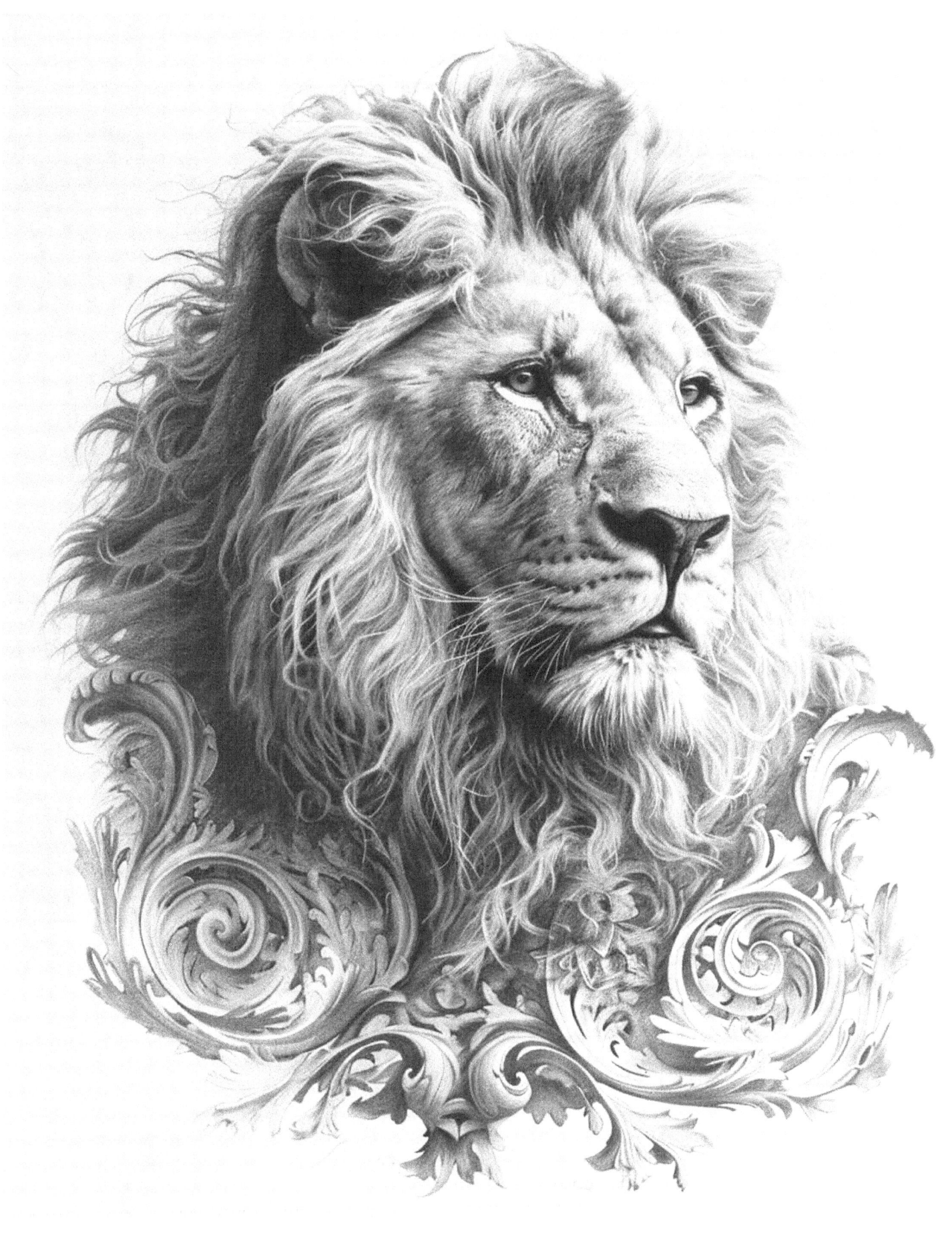

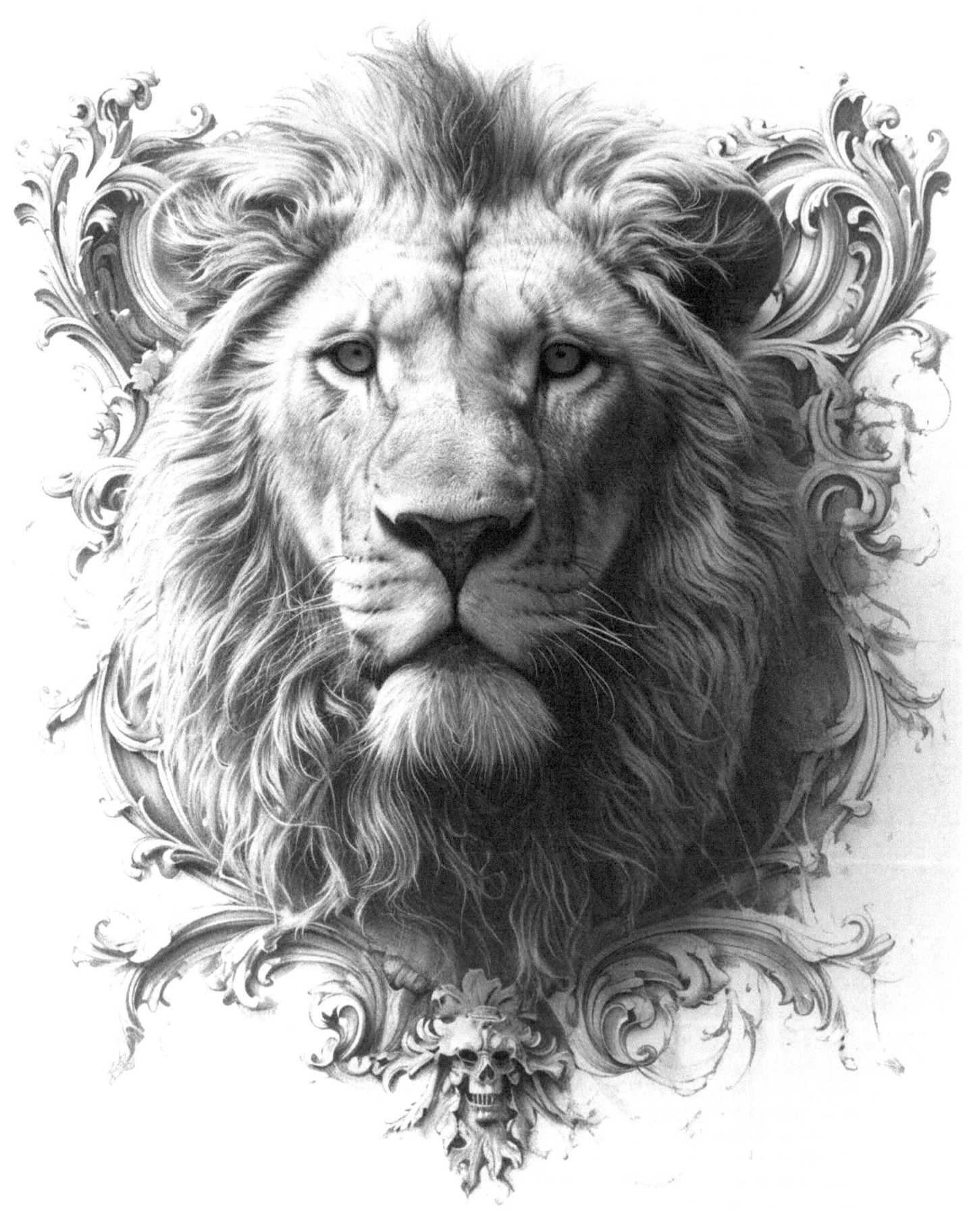

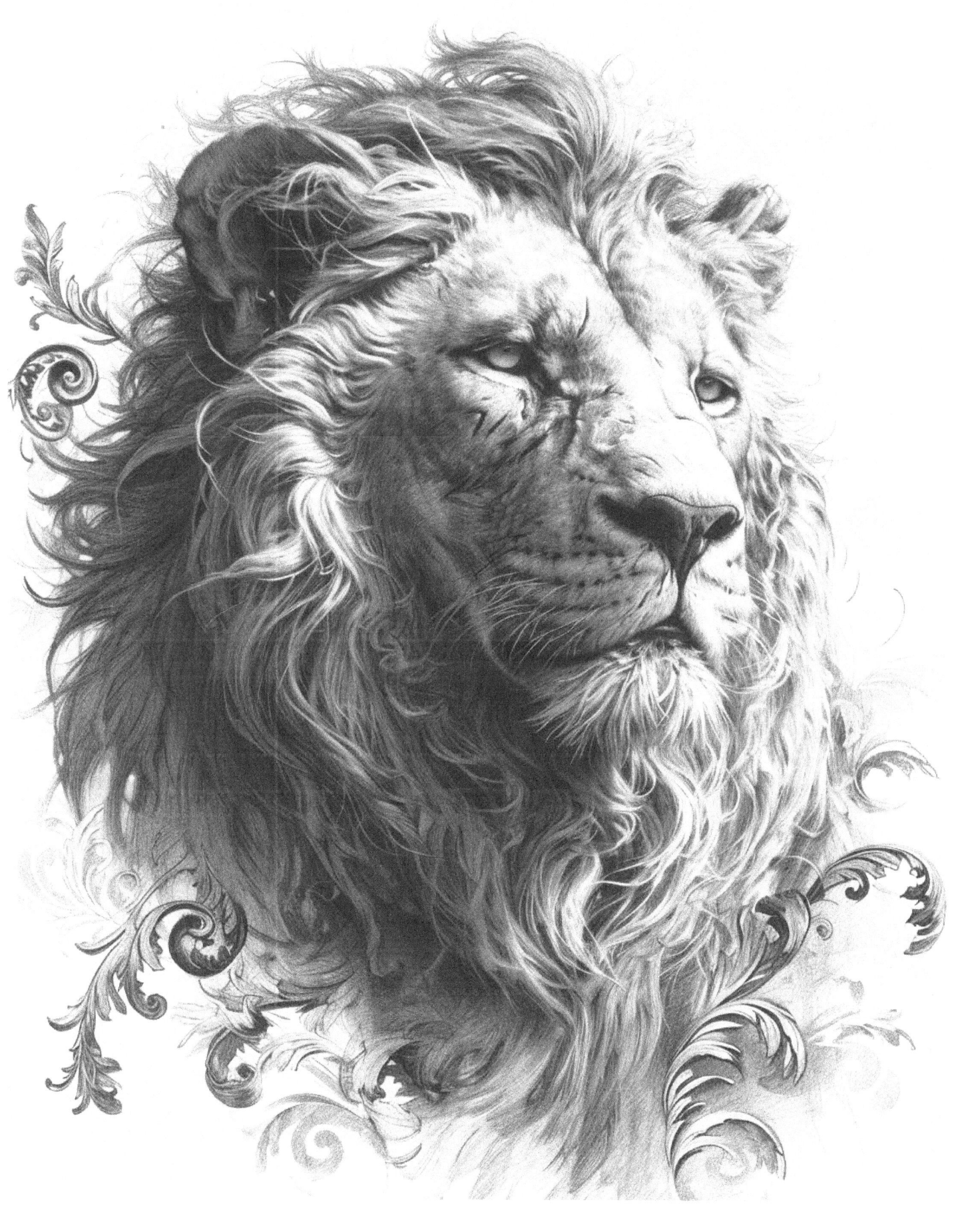

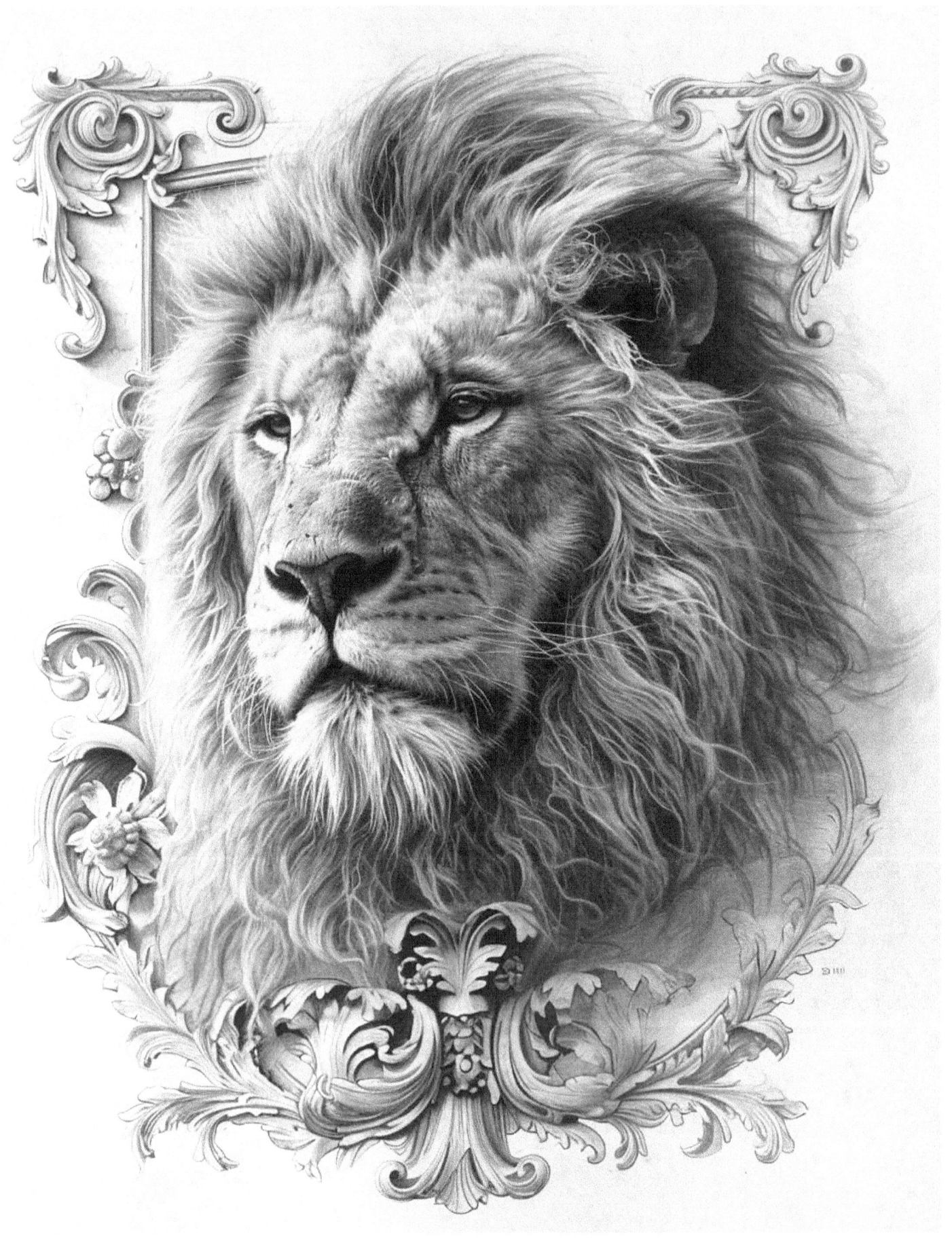

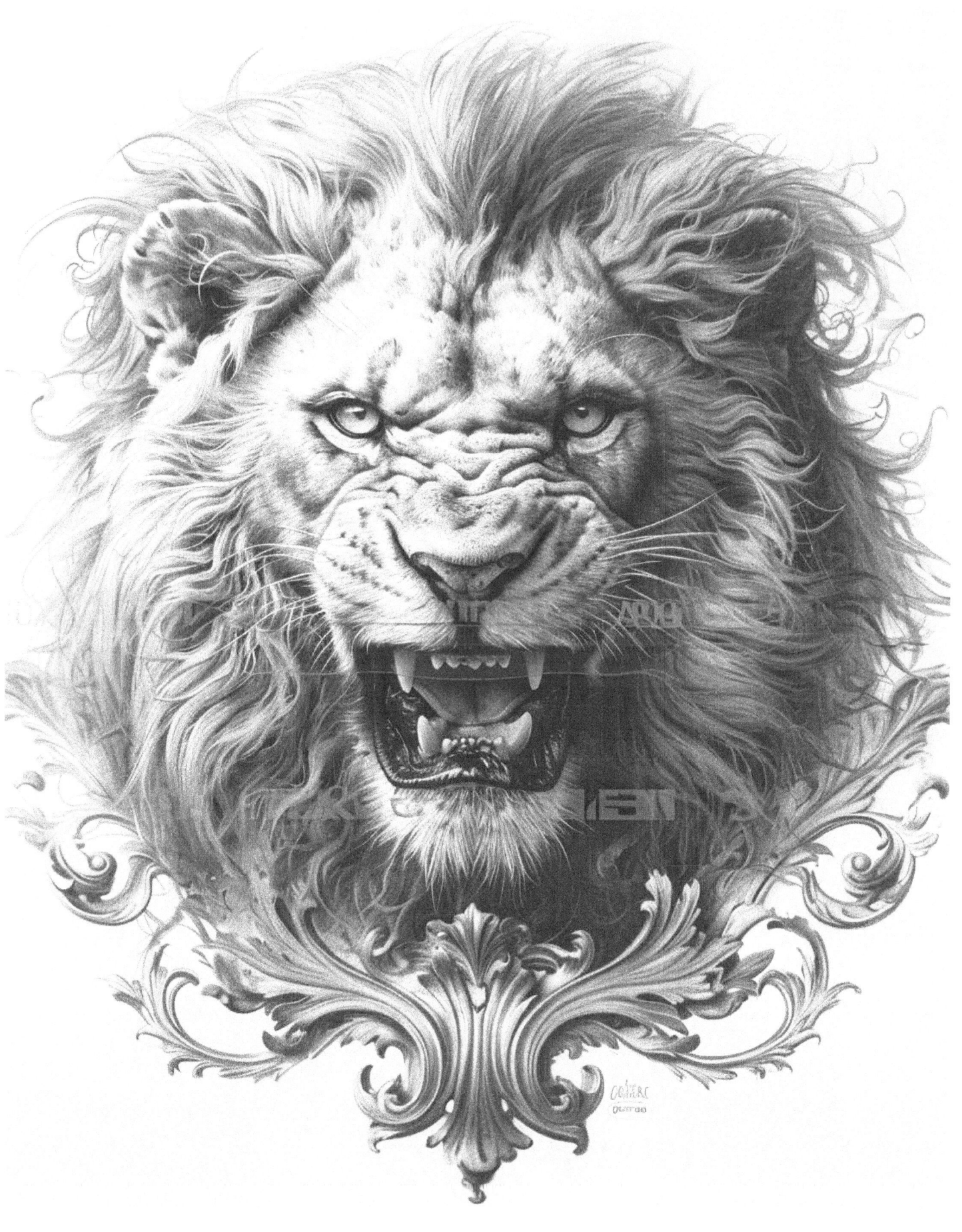

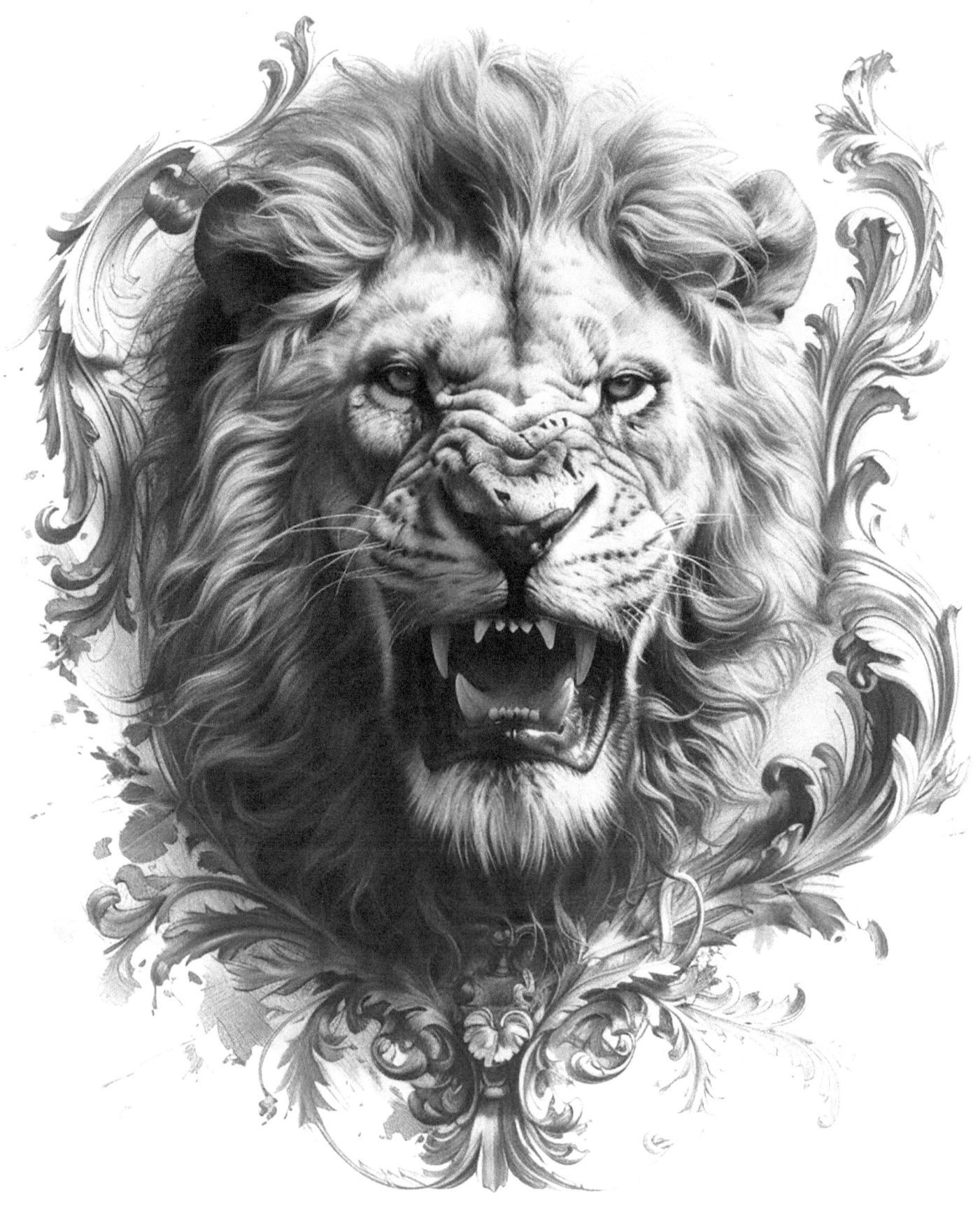

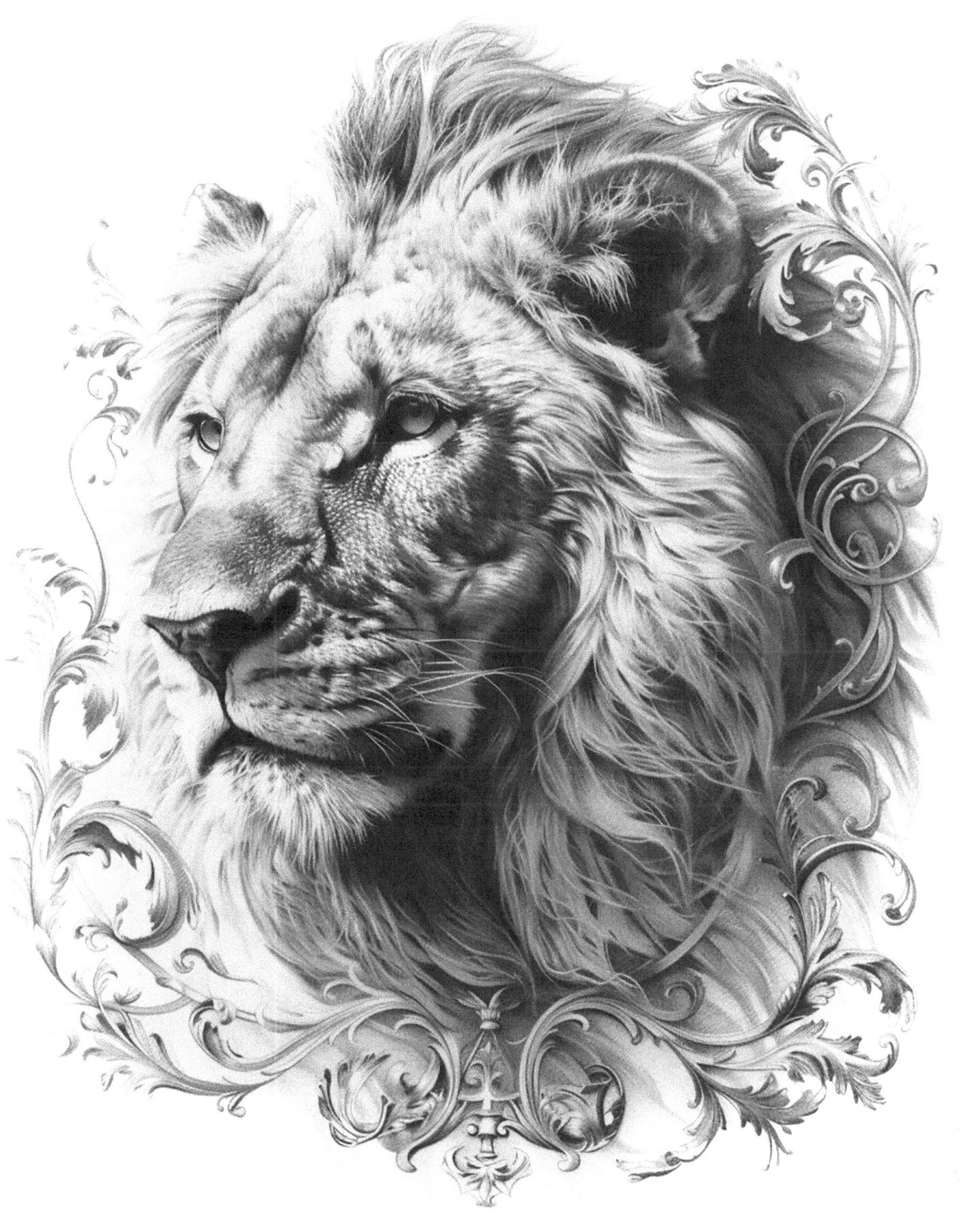

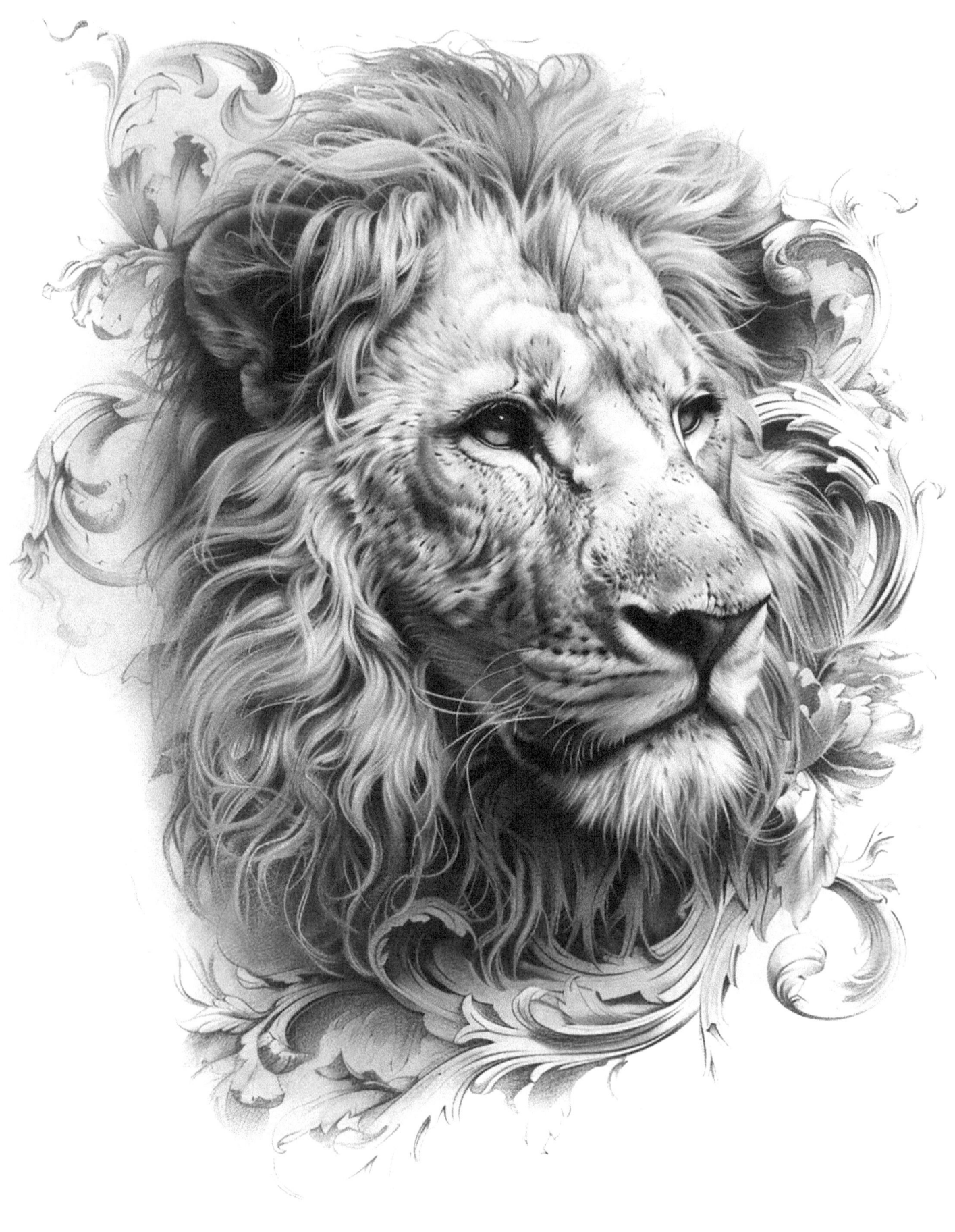

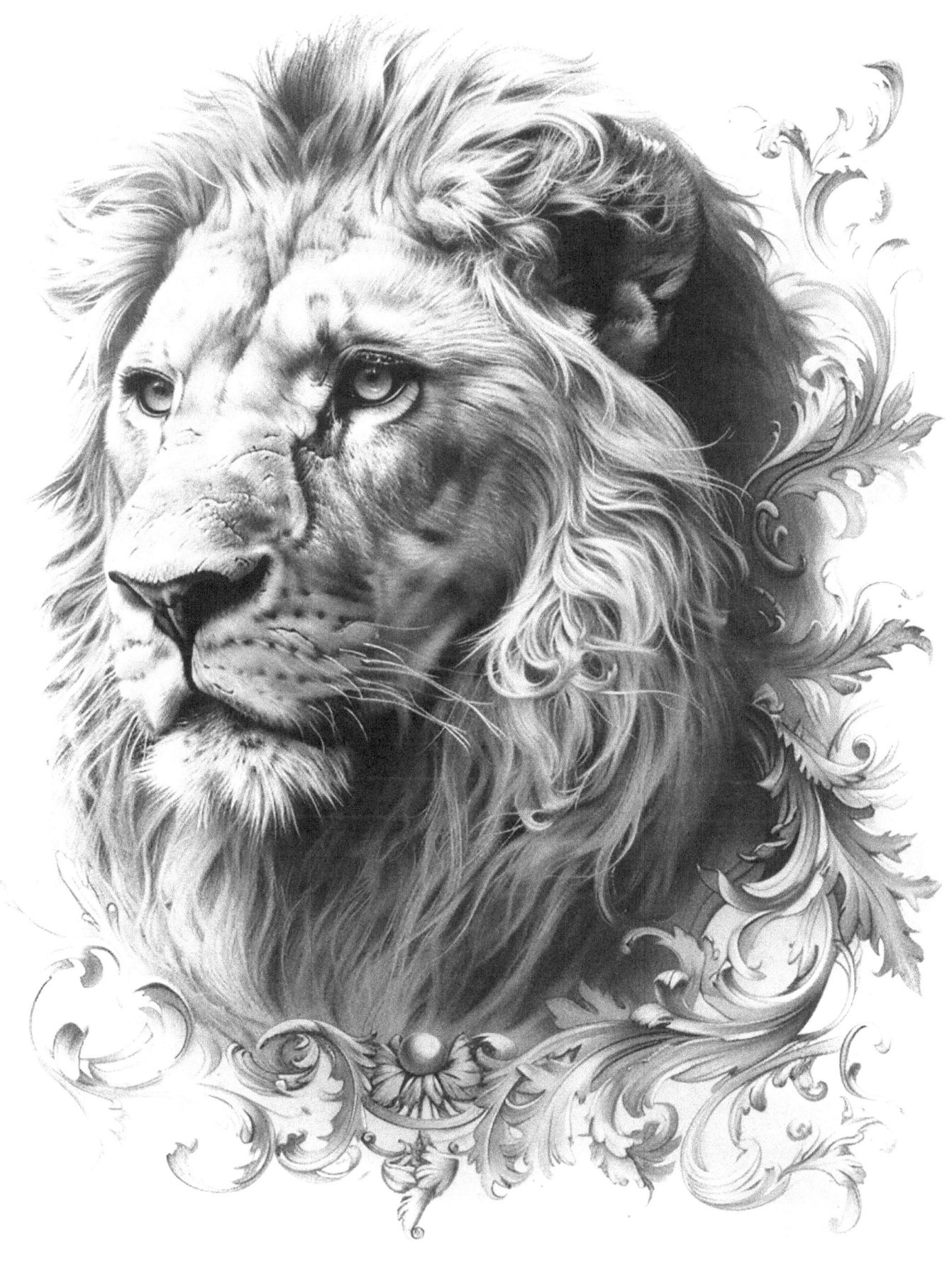

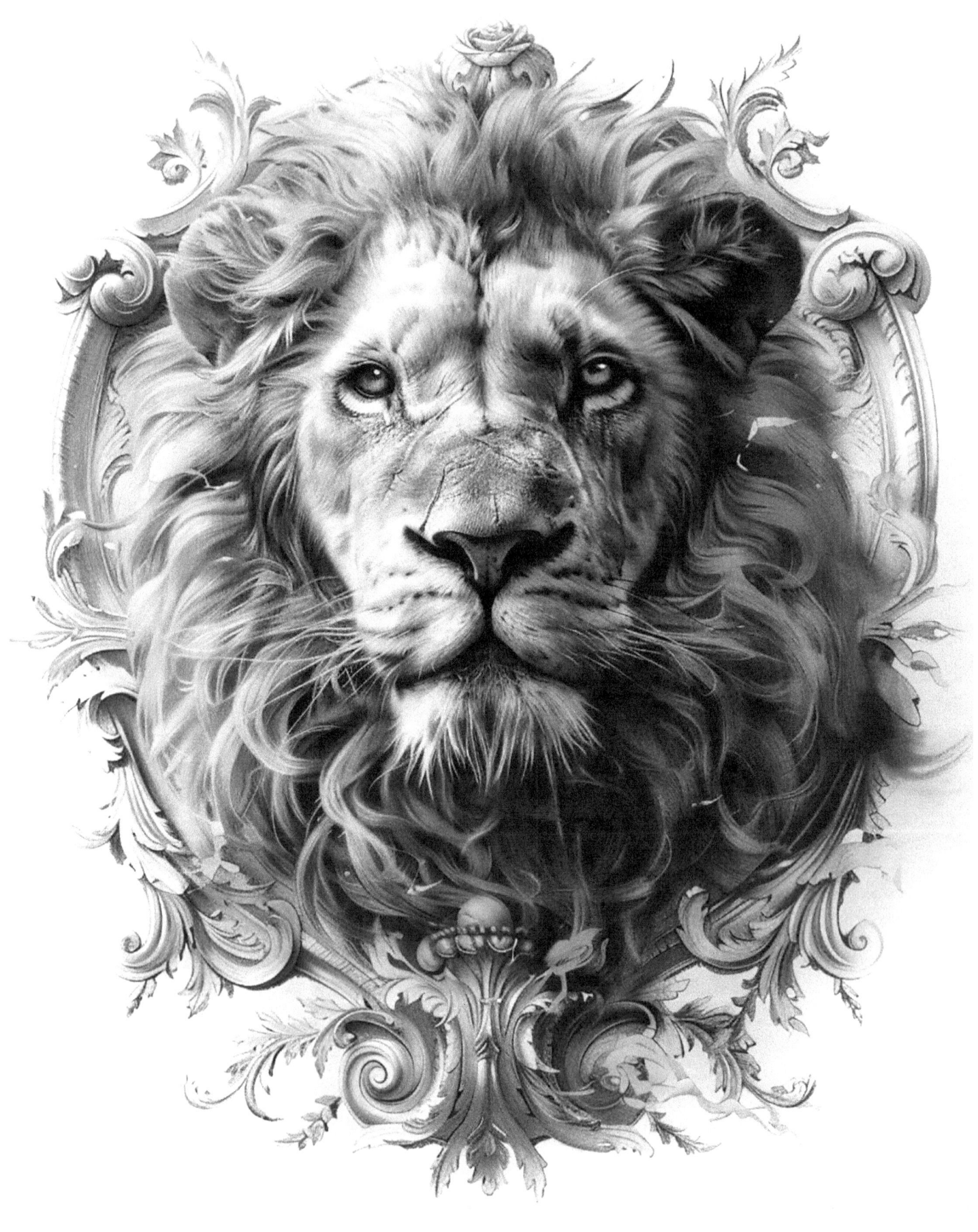

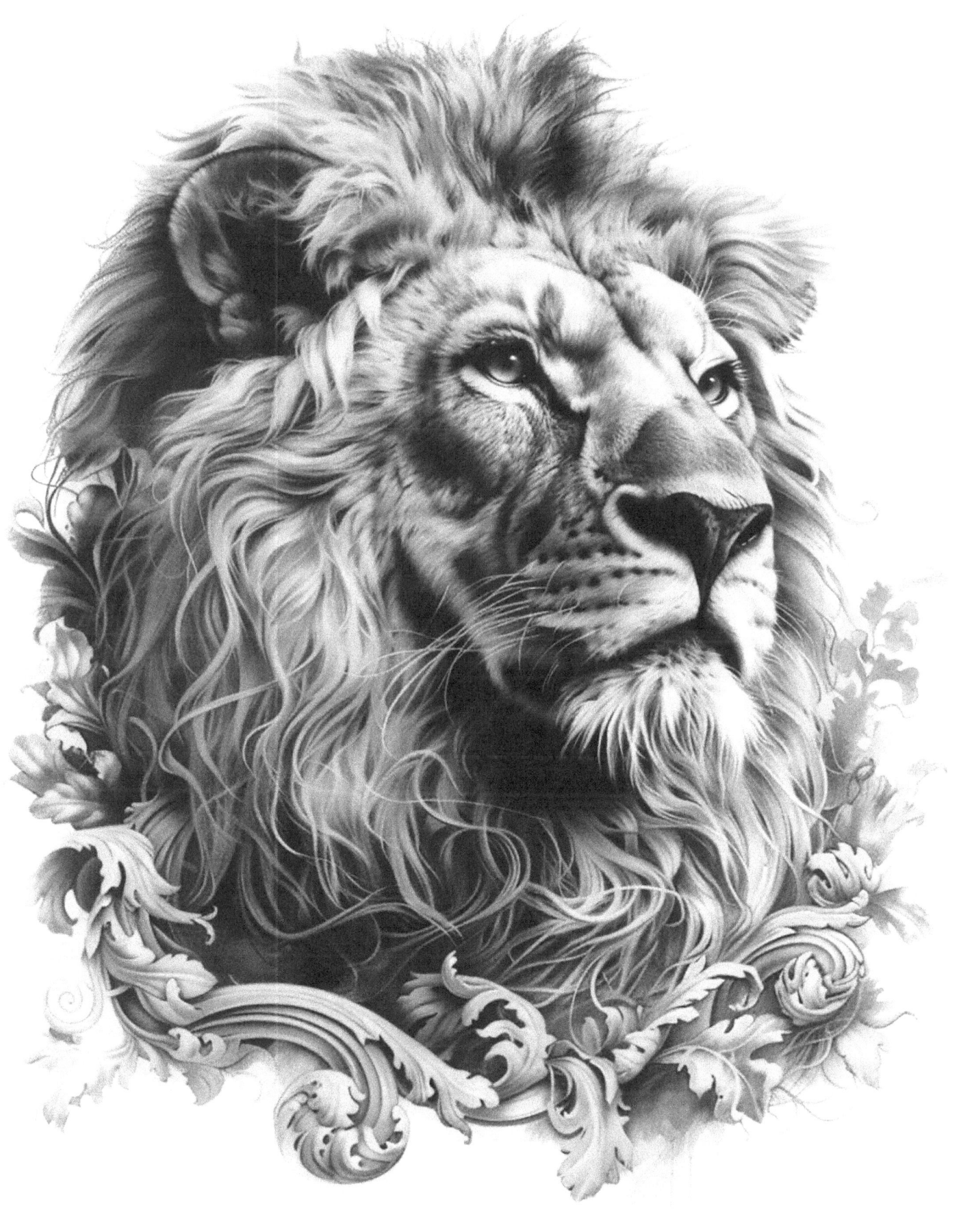

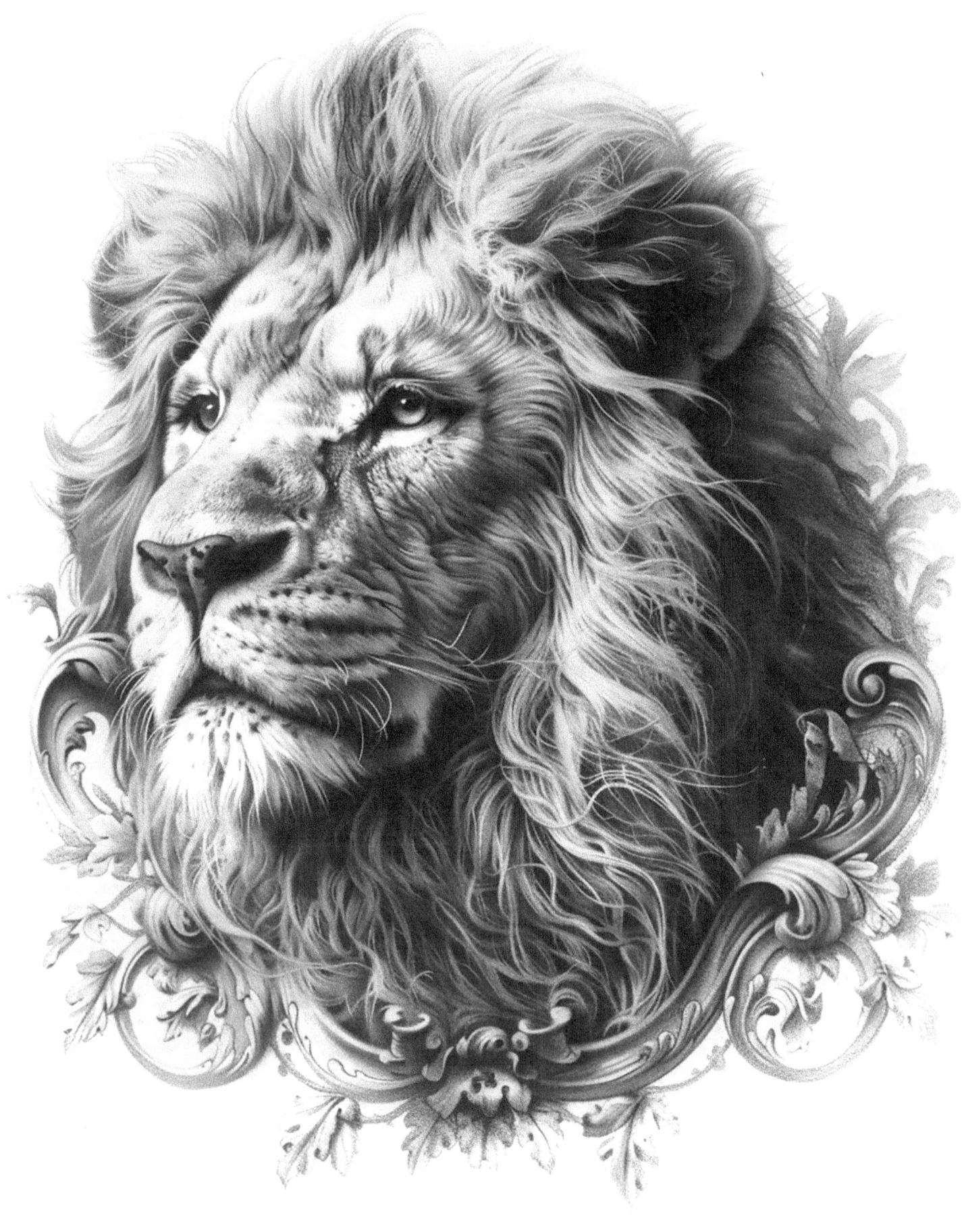

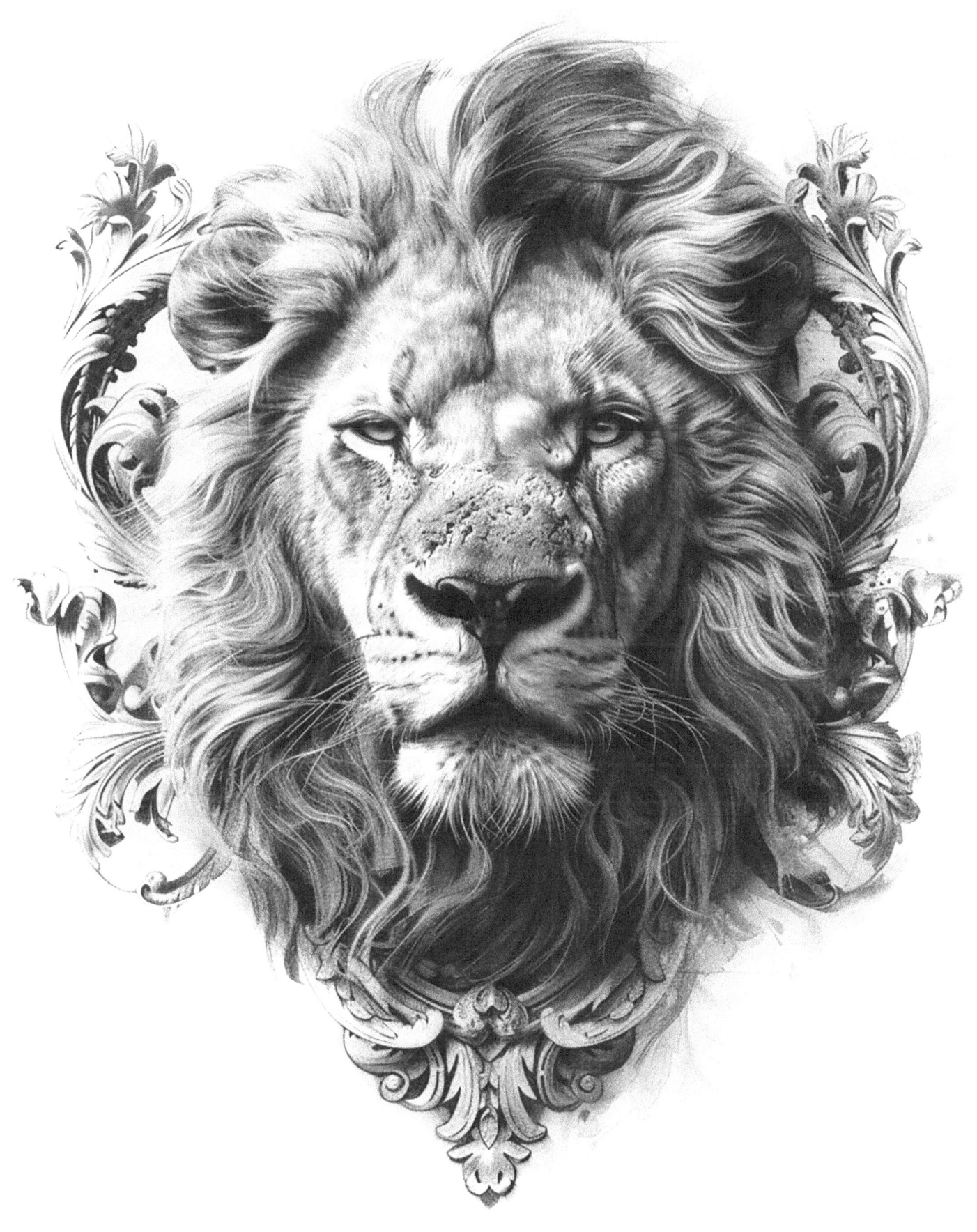

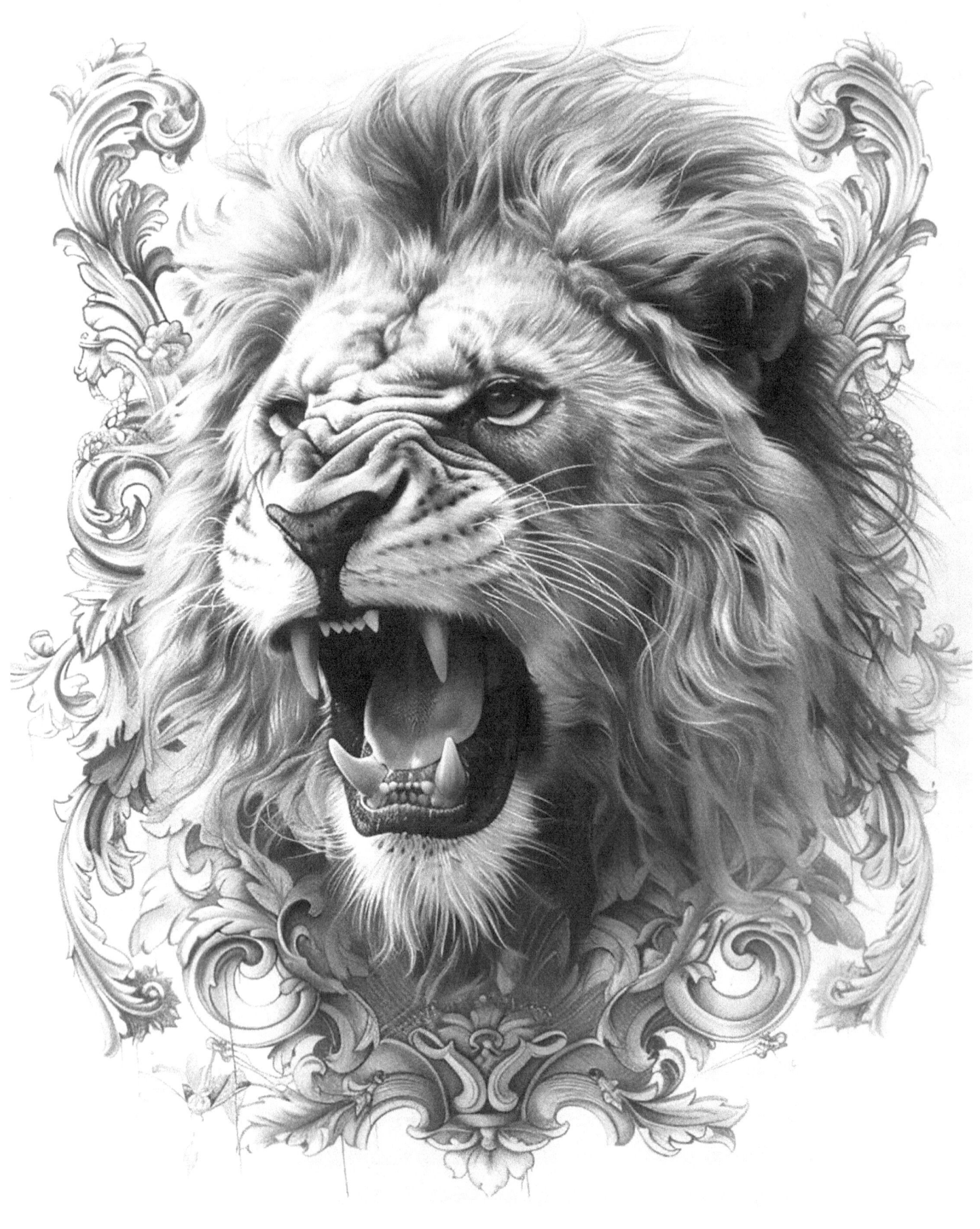

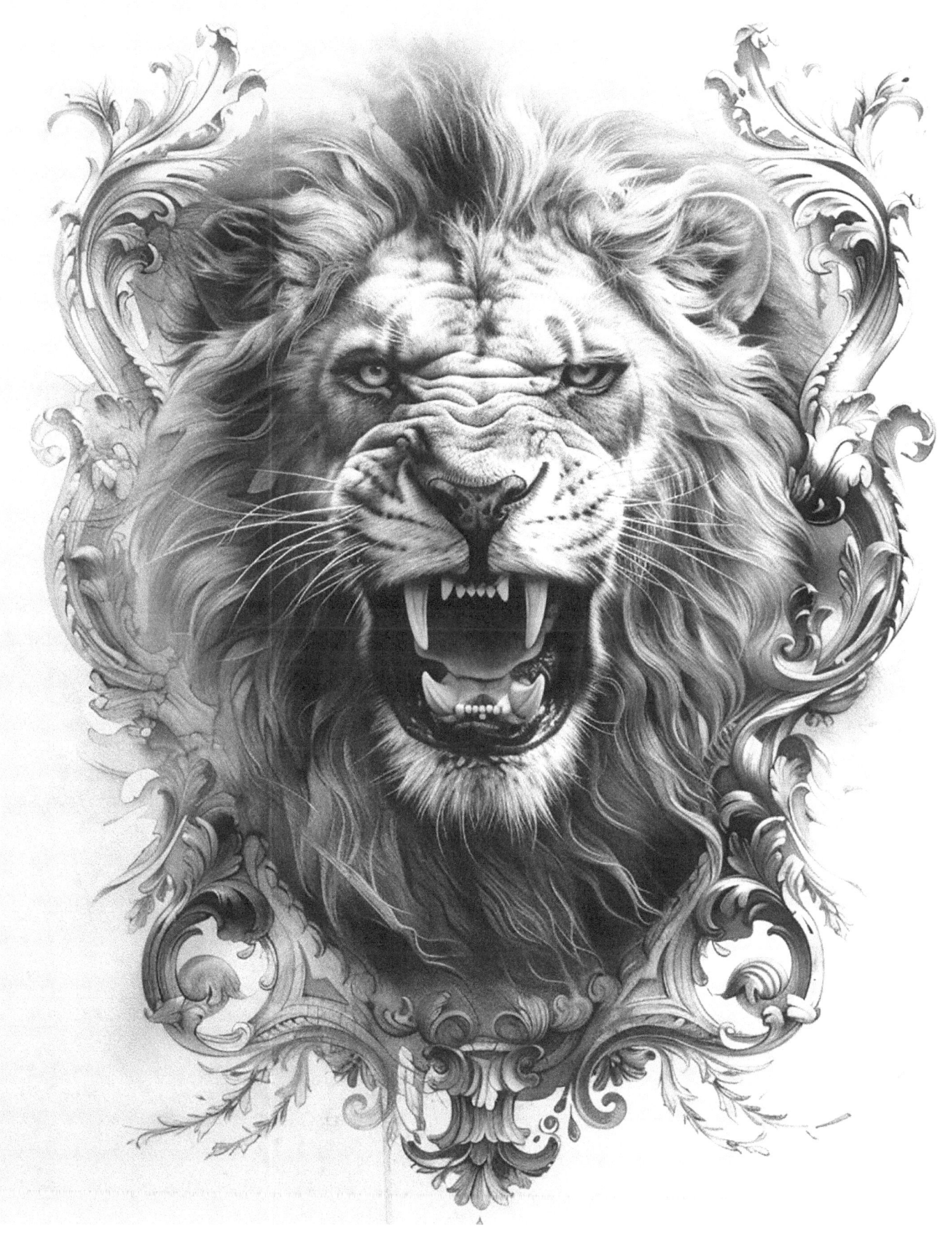

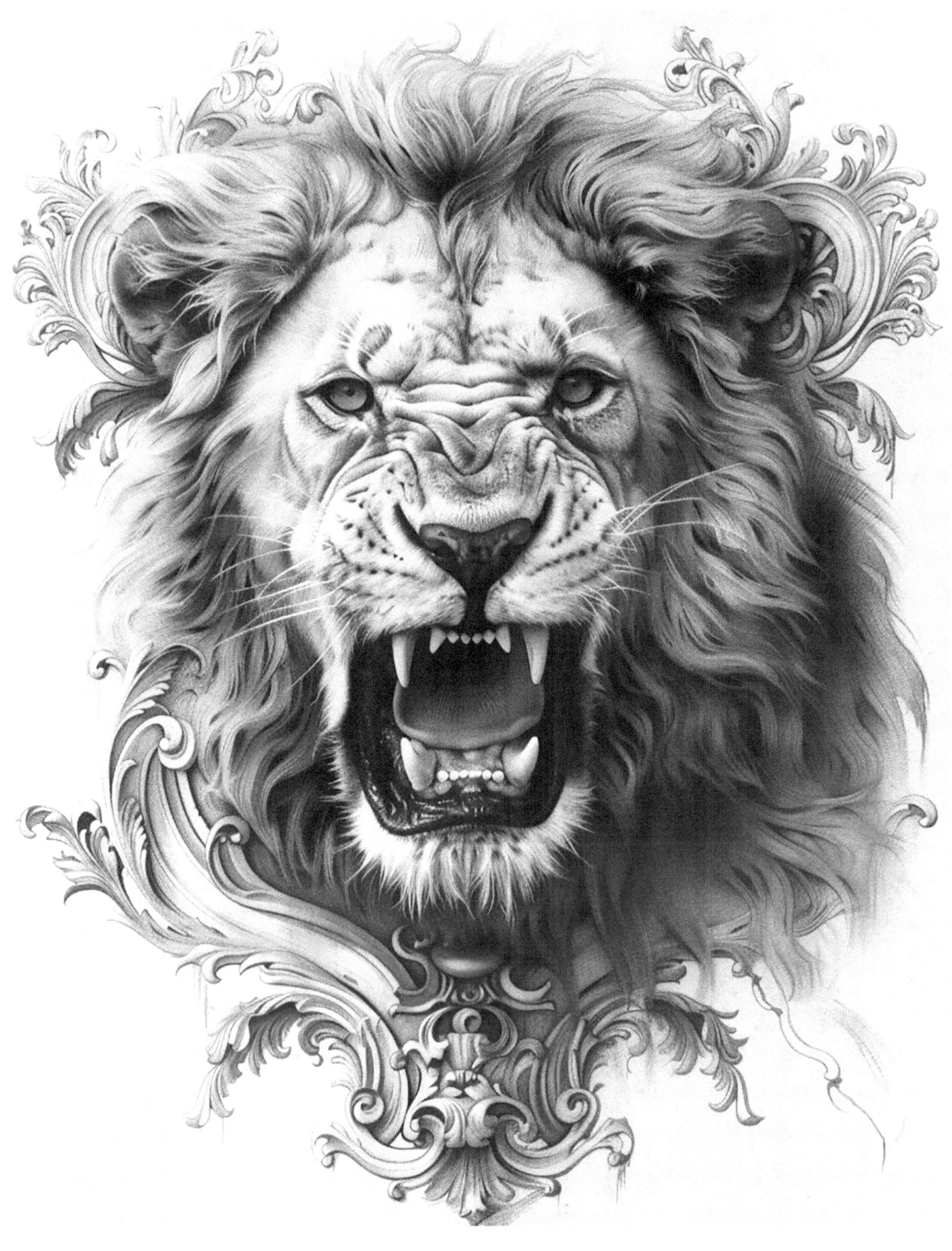

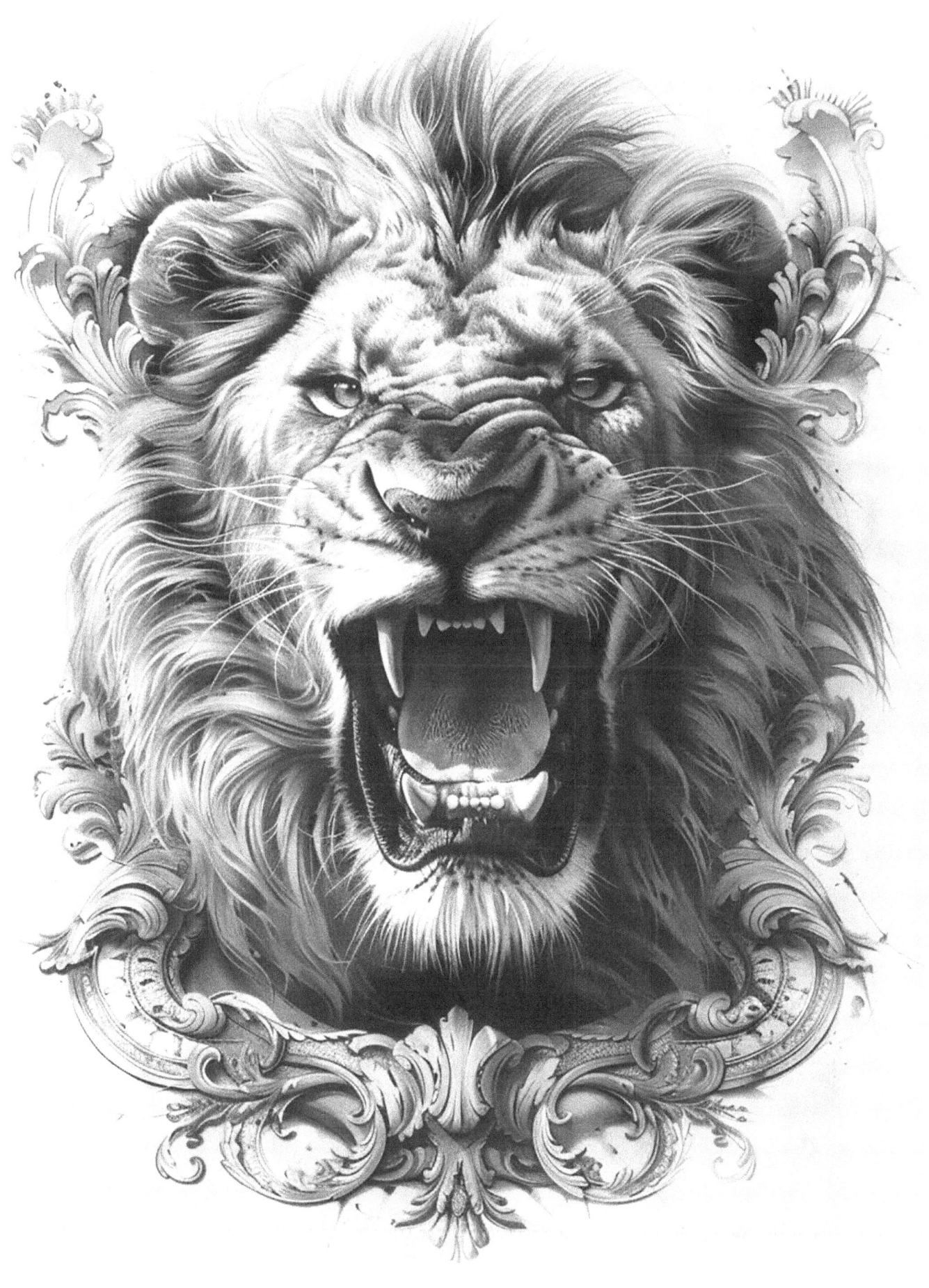

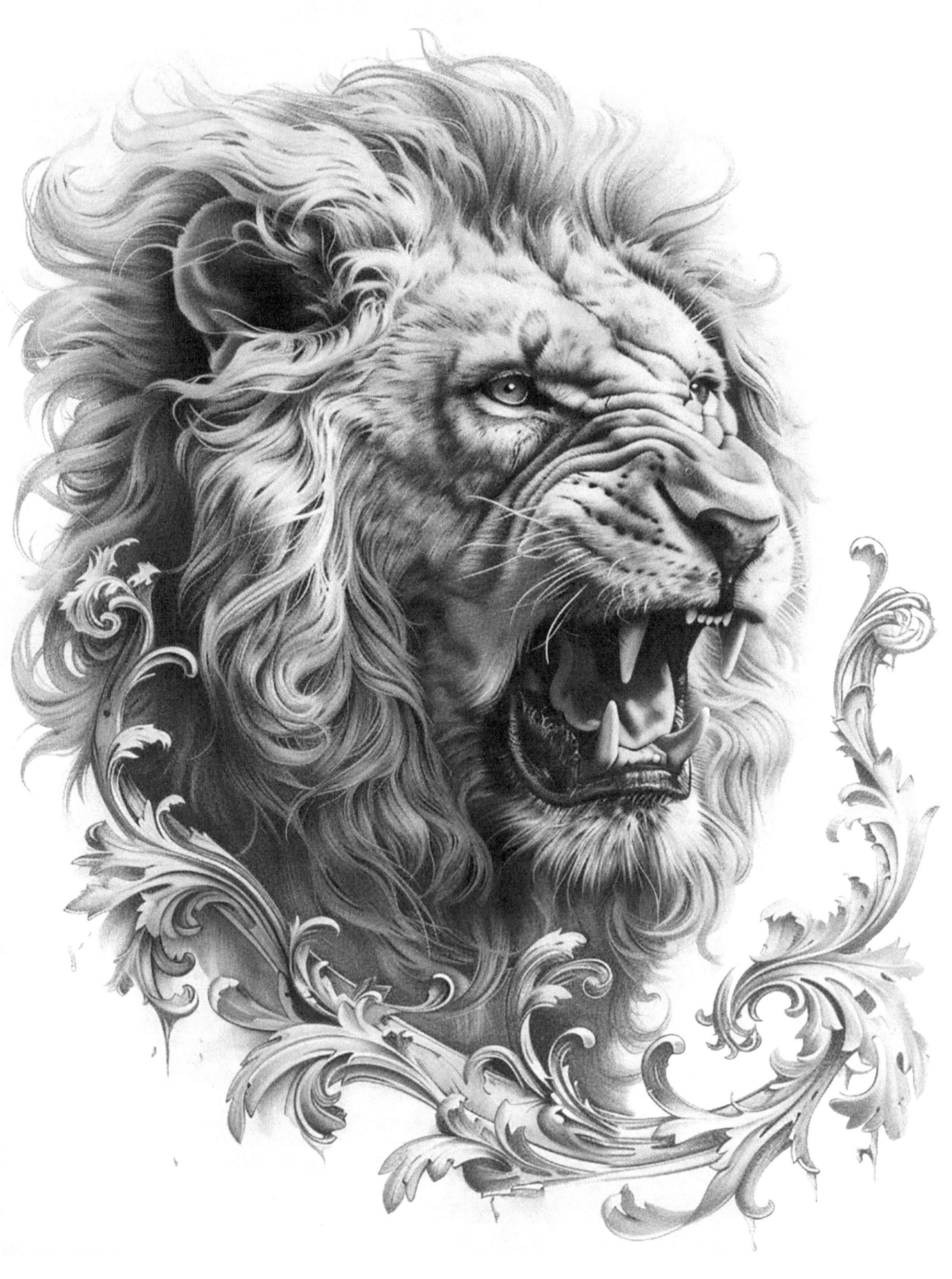

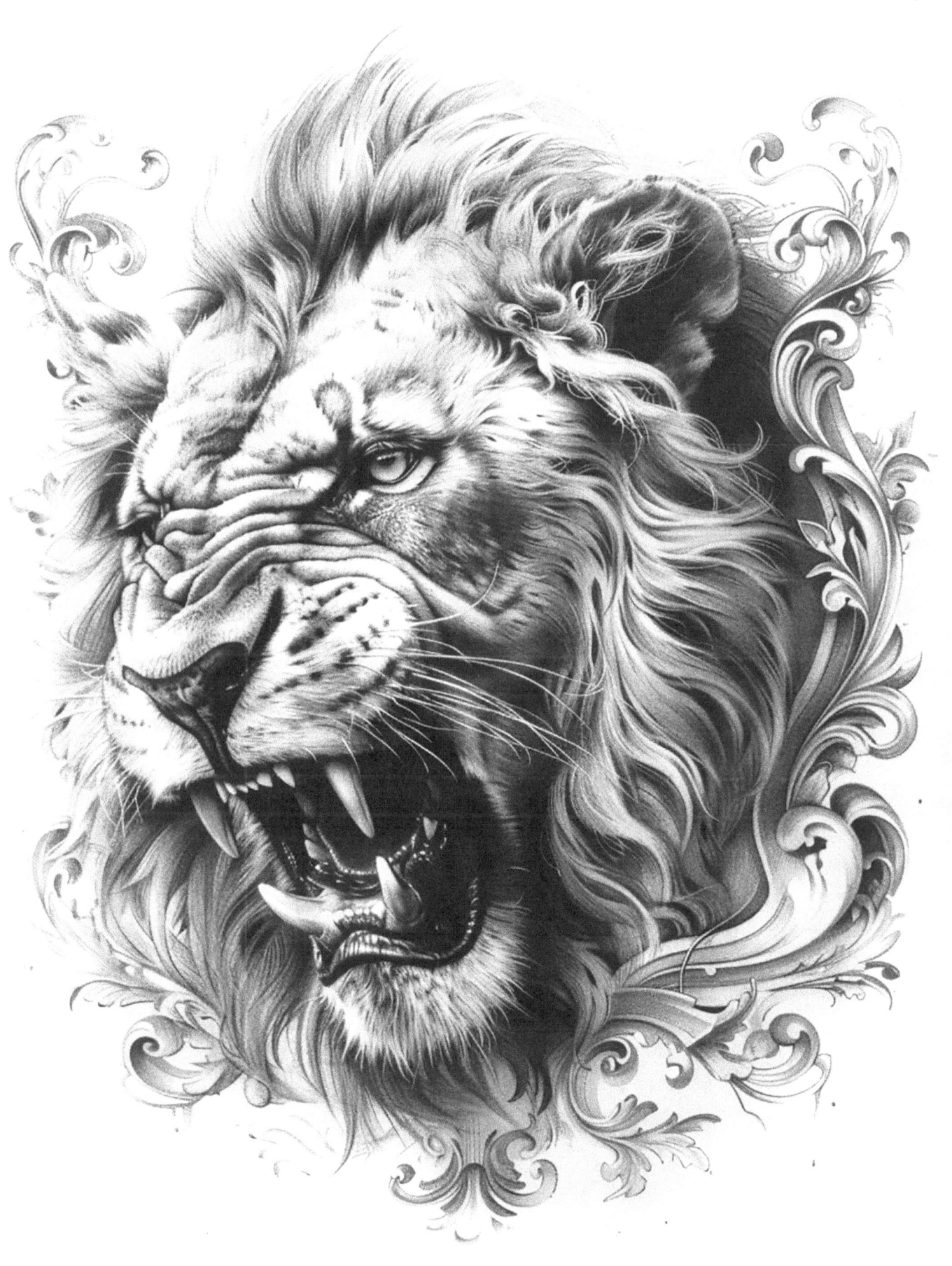

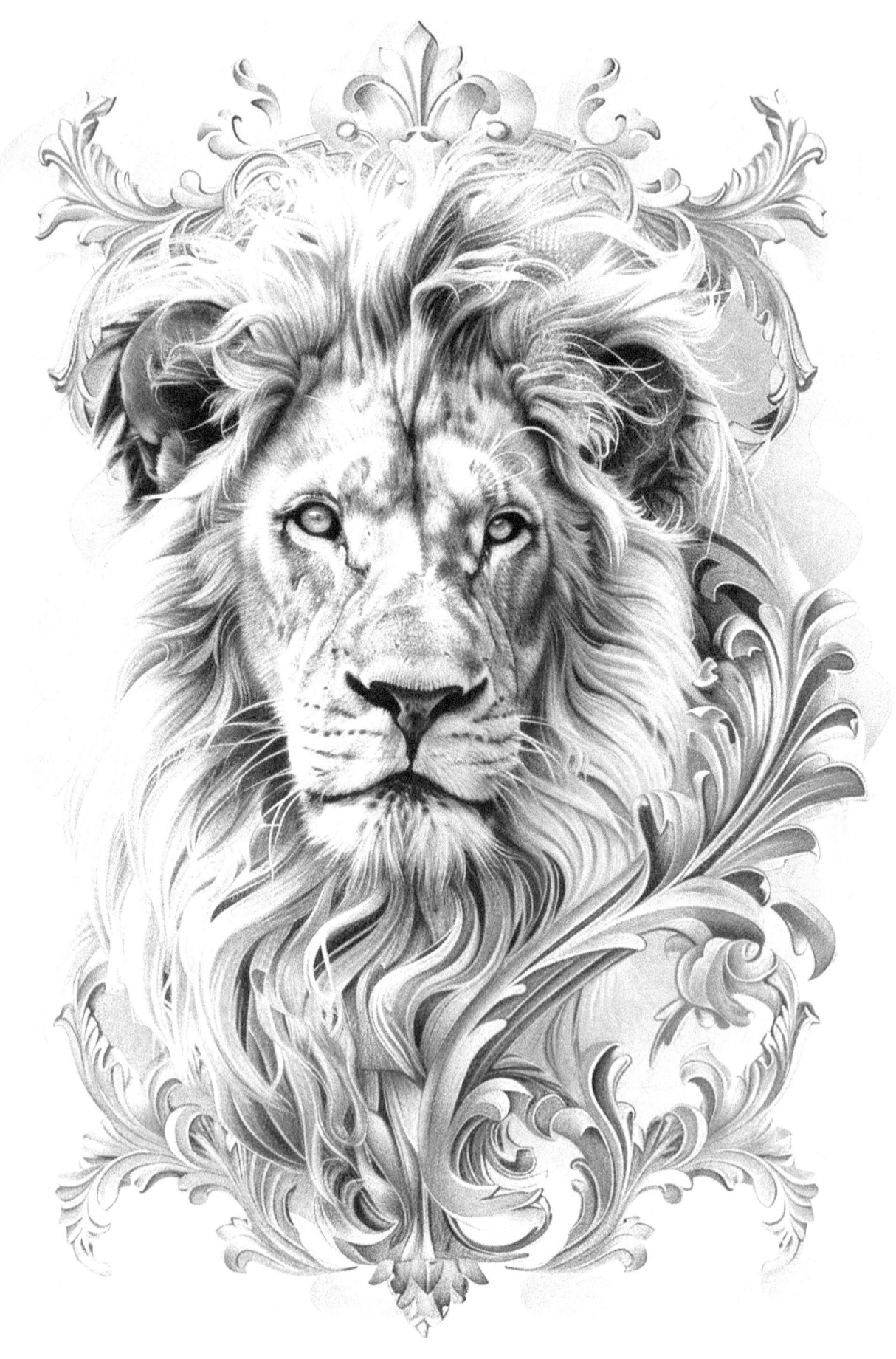

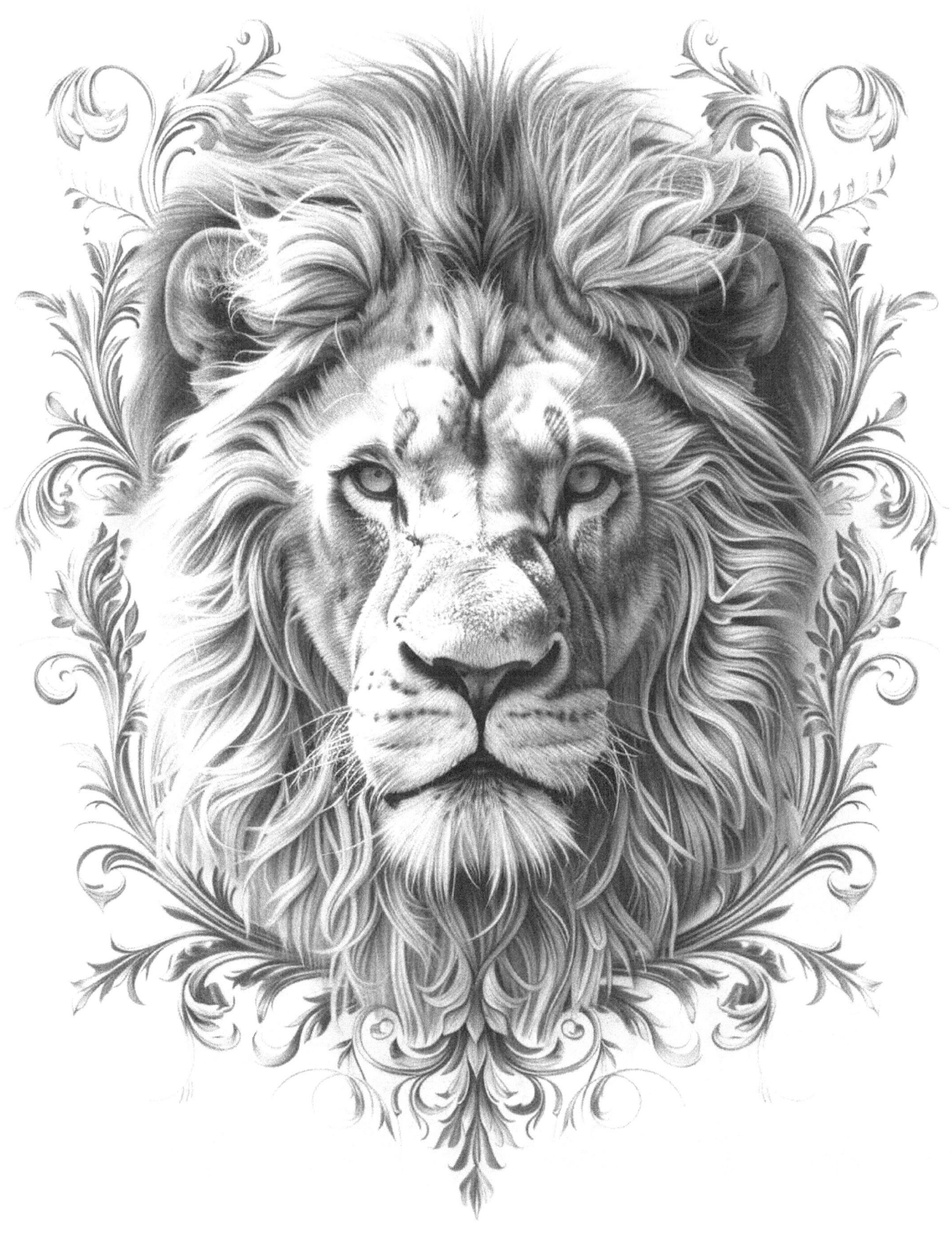

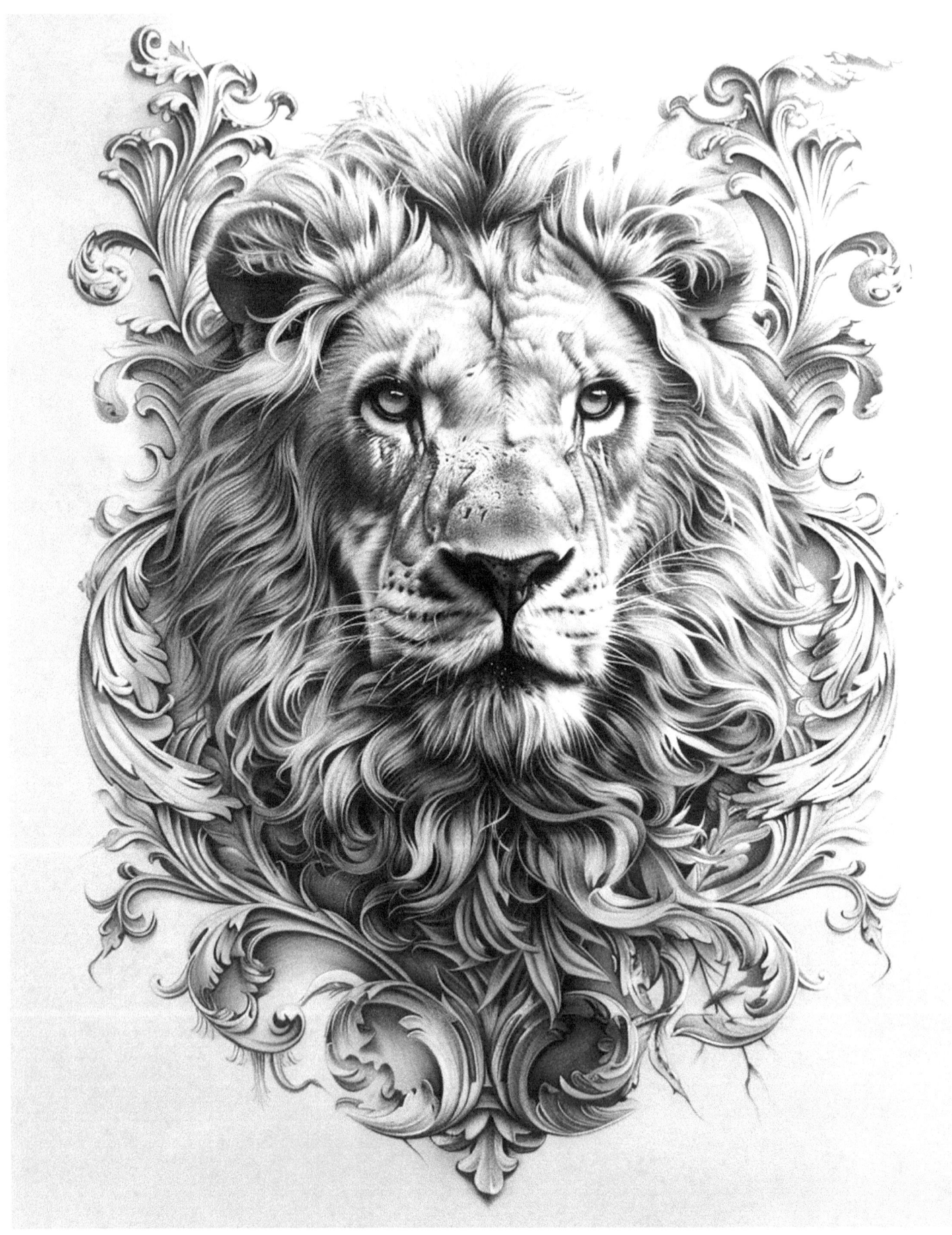

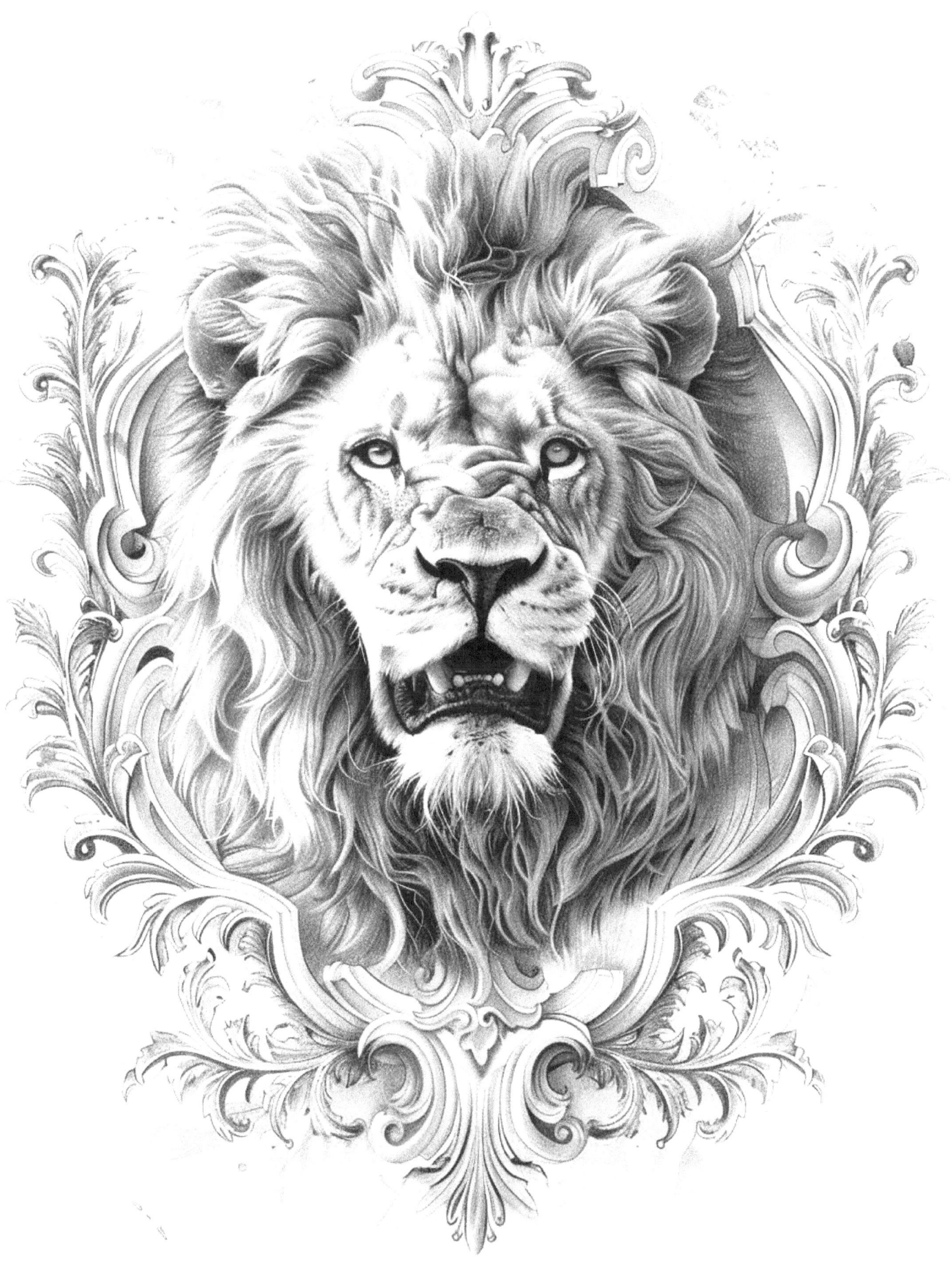

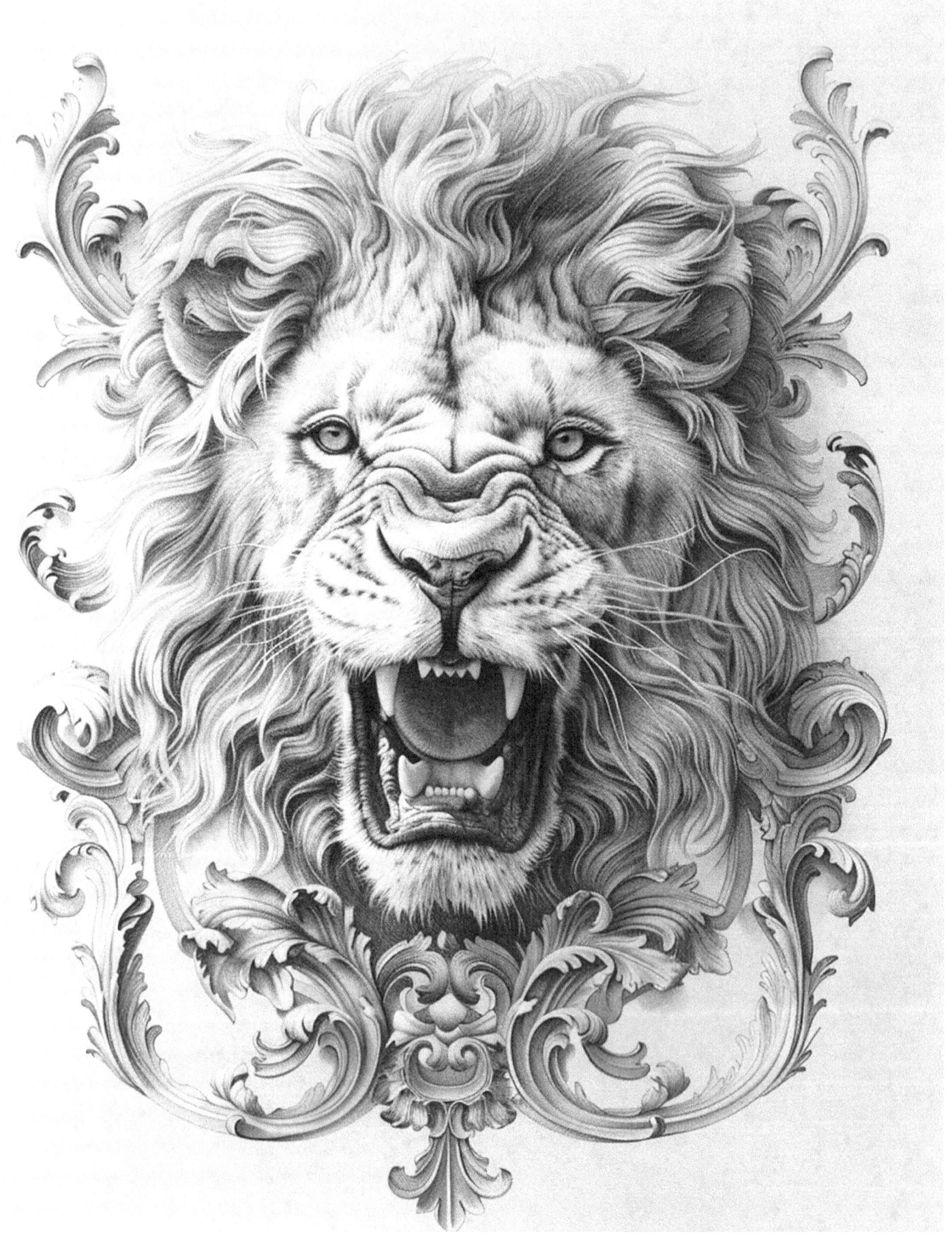

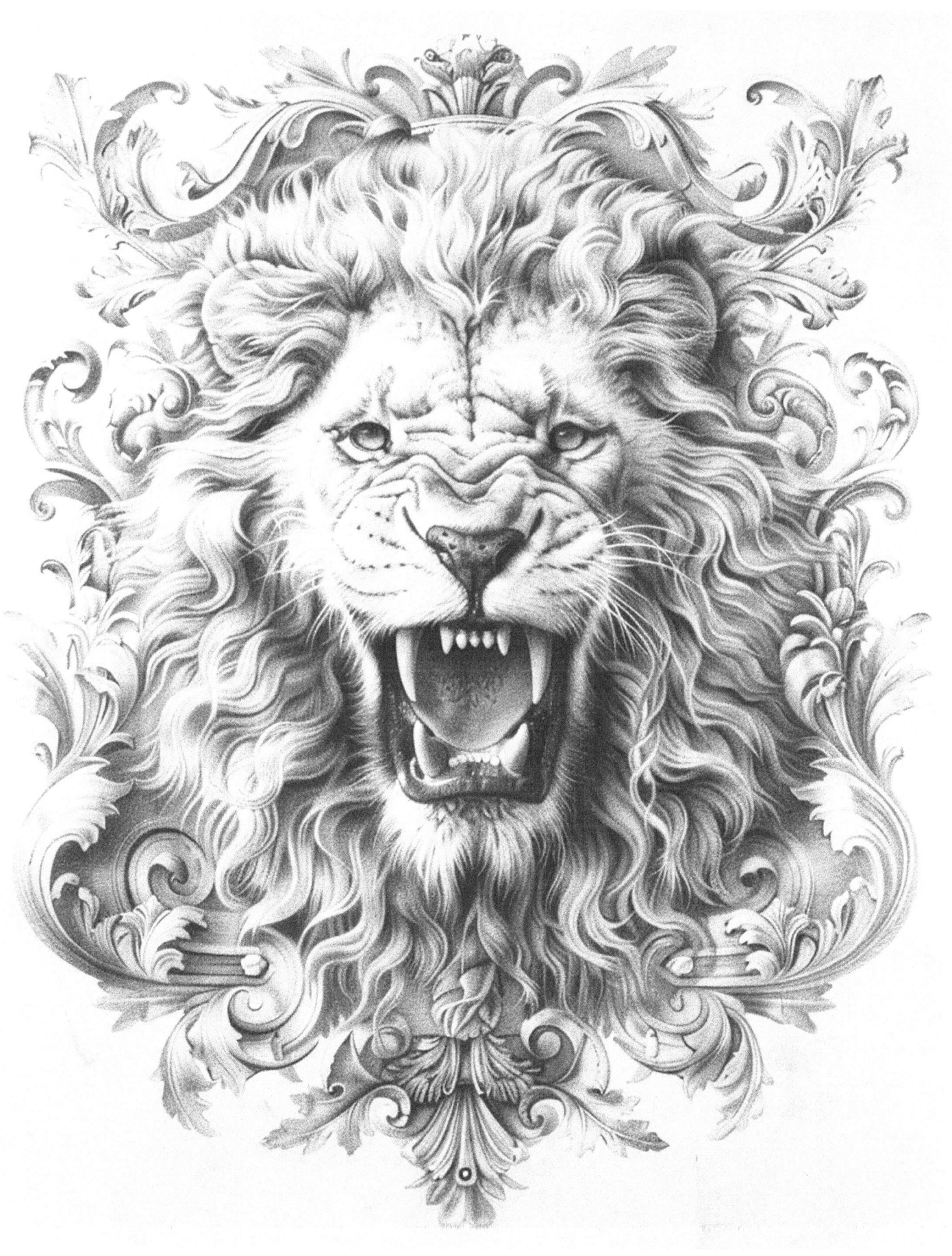

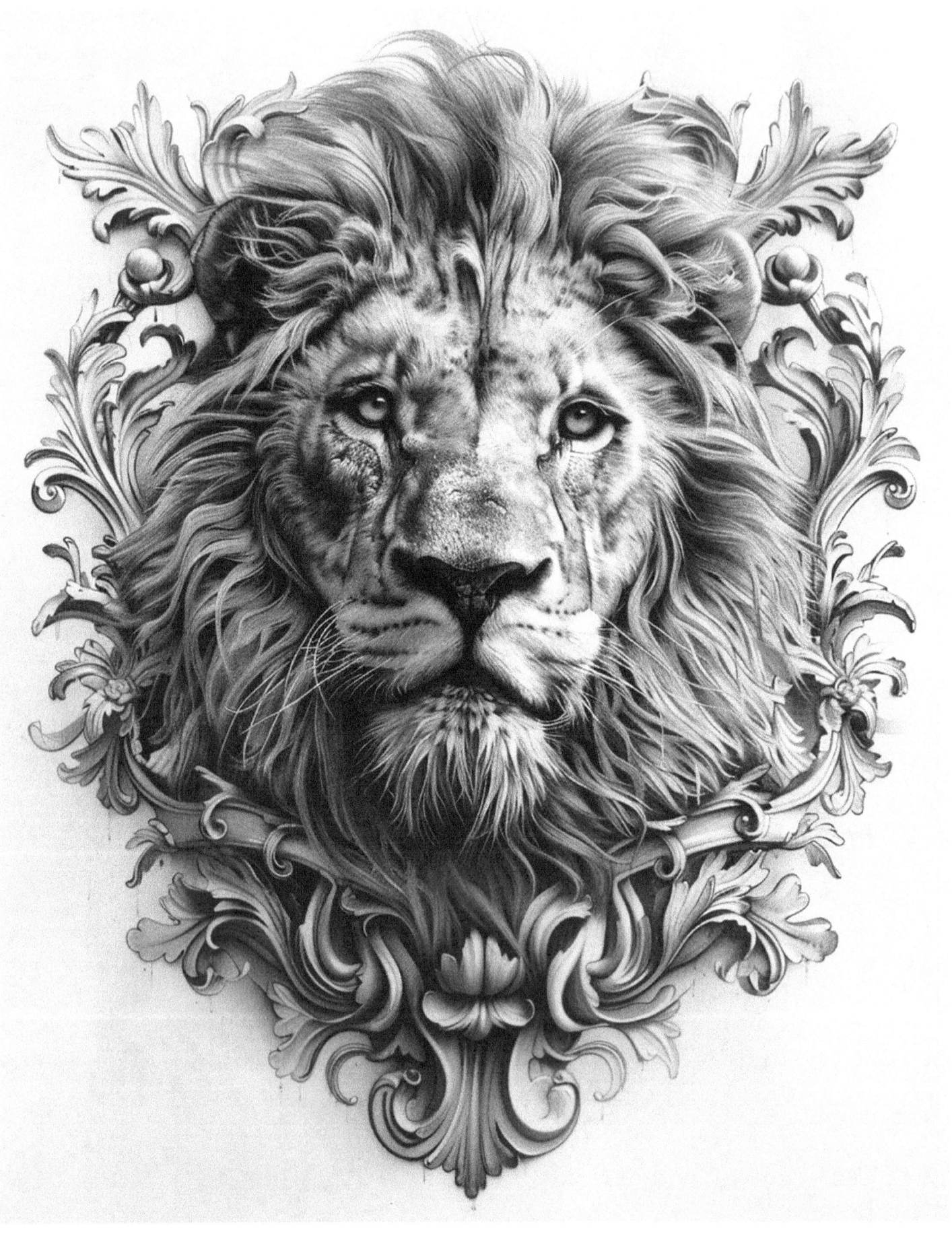

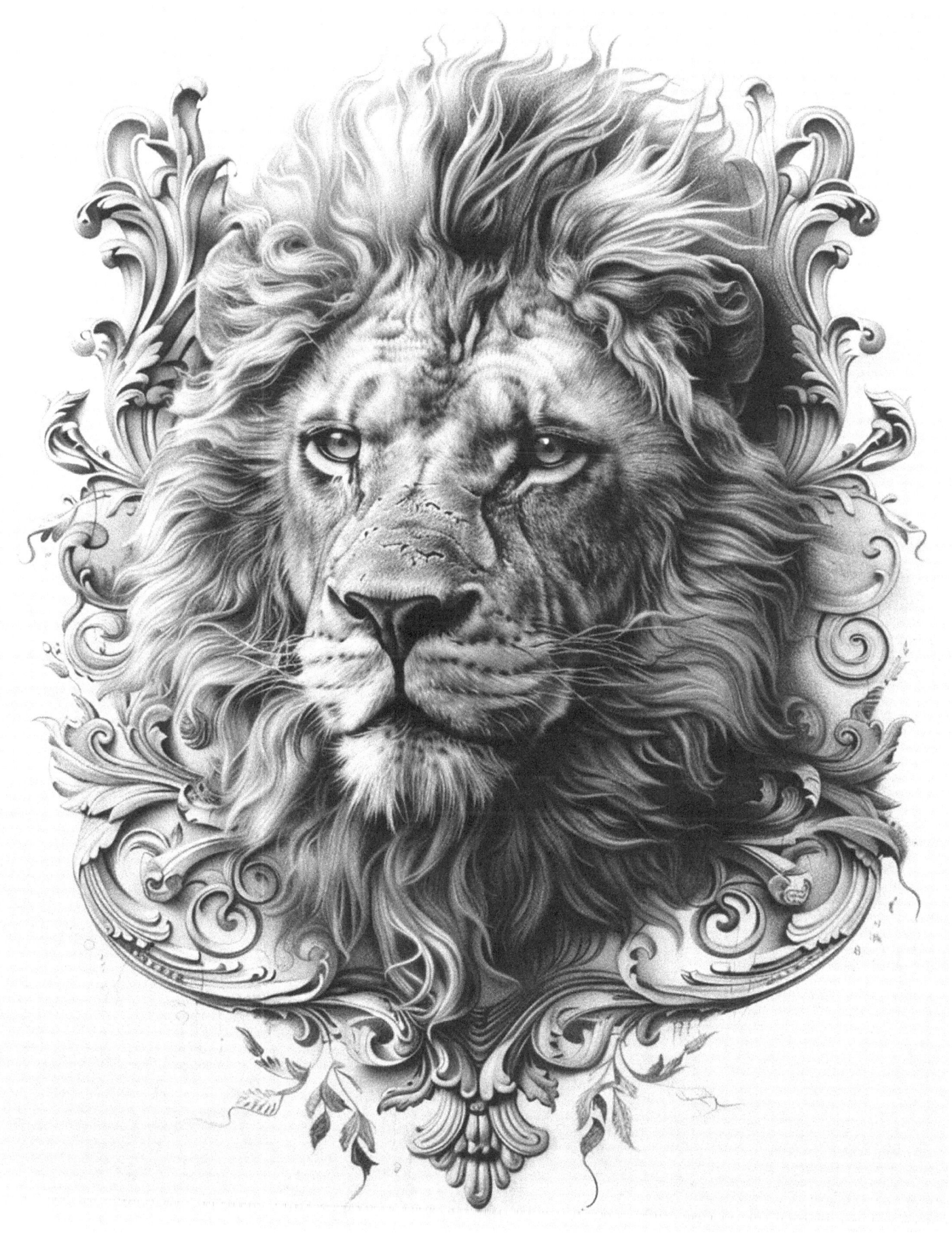

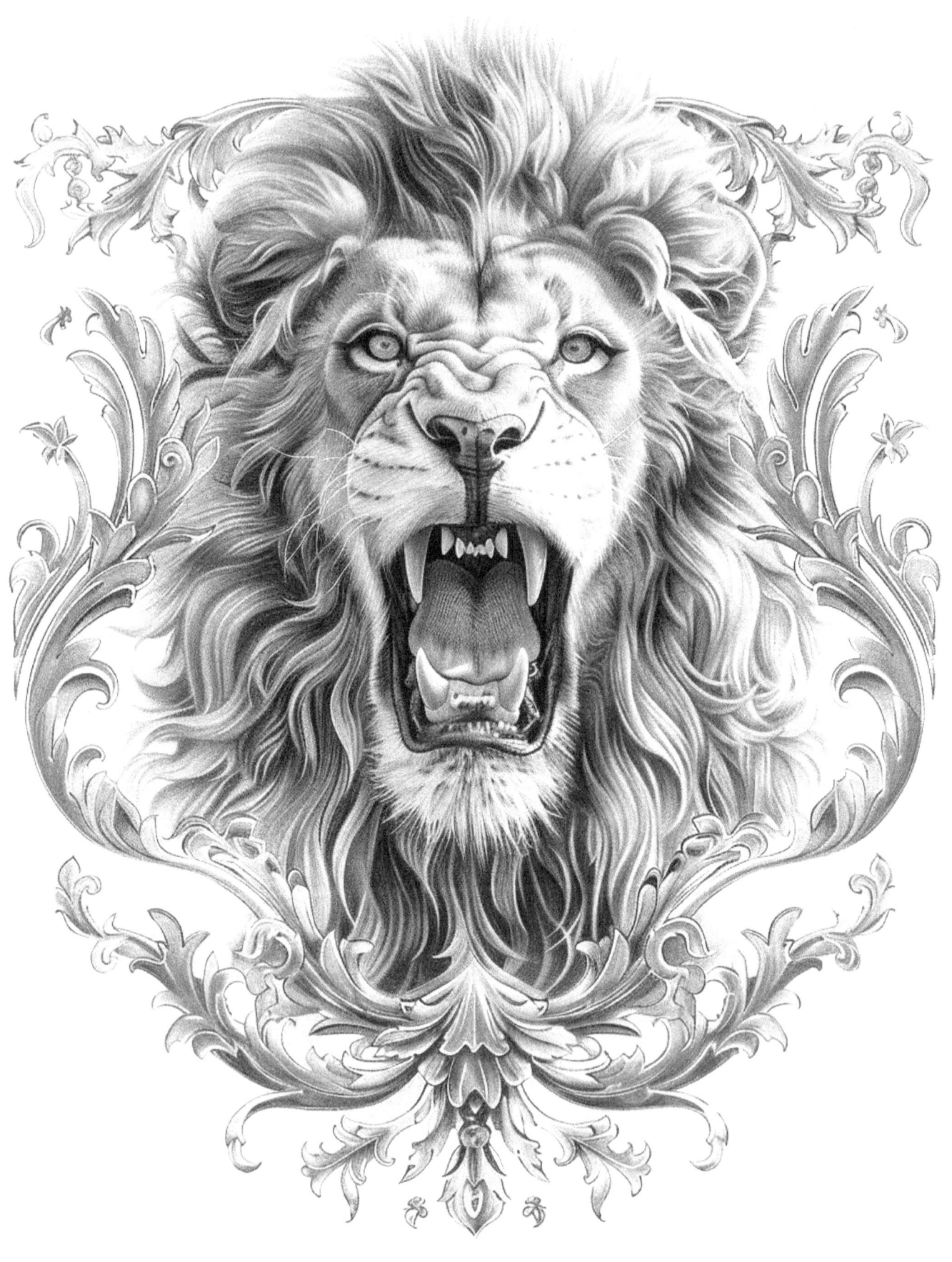

www.ingramcontent.com/pod-product-compliance
Lightning Source LLC
Chambersburg PA
CBHW082245310526
45795CB00015B/2980